Communicating with children and adults

Communicating with children and adults

**INTERPERSONAL SKILLS FOR
EARLY YEARS AND PLAY WORK**

Second edition

Pat Petrie PhD

A member of the Hodder Headline Group
LONDON • SYDNEY • AUCKLAND

First published in Great Britain in 1989
Second edition published in 1997 by
Arnold, a member of the Hodder Headline Group,
338 Euston Road, London NW1 3BH

Whilst the advice and information in this book is believed to be true and
accurate at the date of going to press, neither the author nor the publisher
can accept any legal responsibility or liability for any errors or omissions
that may be made.

British Library Cataloguing-in-Publication Data
A catalogue record for this book is available from the British Library

Library of Congress Cataloging-in-Publication Data
A catalog record for this book is available from the Library of Congress

ISBN 0 340 65257 8

Typeset in 10/12 Palatino by Paul Bennett, Tonbridge
Printed and bound in Great Britain by J.W. Arrowsmith Ltd, Bristol

Contents

Acknowledgements

I wish to thank all the people who have contributed to this book: the play workers, nursery staff and childminders who have told me about their experiences and let me see them at work; Barbara Tizard for permission to use exerpts from her recordings of children's talk; Rachel Pinney and Sally Maxwell for letting me observe them doing 'special times'; Jane Lane and Bob Hughes for their advice. None of the above is responsible for any errors of judgement in the book!

I must especially acknowledge the National Nursery Examination Board (NNEB) who supported my work developing interpersonal skills training. This book is an extension and adaptation of that approach, making it available to a wider group of students and practitioners in early years and play work.

The publishers would like to thank the staff and children of Tottenham Green Under-fives Centre and Nketewa Day Nursery for their assistance in allowing the photographs used in this book to be taken there; Collins Publishers for their permission to use material from *Young Children Learning* by Tizard and Hughes (Fontana, 1984); Barnaby's Picture Library for the photographs reproduced on pages 10–11; John Birdsall for the photograph on page 10 (bottom right); and Harry Venning for the illustrations.

Introduction

This second edition of *Communicating with Children and Adults* is for all those who work or intend to work with children, both early years workers and play workers. It covers many different work settings, including nurseries, playgroups, childminders, special needs units, adventure playgrounds, kids' clubs, after-school and holiday playschemes. It enlarges on the first edition, which was intended mainly for people working with under fives.

The subject of the book is interpersonal communication, that is, communication that takes place between people, face to face. It is not, therefore, about written communication.

A key feature of the book is that it is about communicating with both children and adults and it uses the same practical and theoretical framework for both groups. People who work with children professionally need to be able to communicate effectively with everyone they meet. Their communications with adults – parents and colleagues – indirectly affect the children they work with. In the children's interests all the adults concerned should be able to communicate and cooperate to the best of their ability; staff who are trained in interpersonal skills can take a lead in this. Communications with the children themselves have a more direct effect, and can either foster or impede a child's emotional and intellectual development. Especially in early years or play work, staff who are skilled interpersonal communicators can encourage the children's own social skills: a desirable outcome of their professional expertise.

Communicating with Children and Adults shows ways in which staff can take responsibility for their own part in any act of communication and at the same time help the other person, child or adult, to communicate effectively. Most of the chapters examine one aspect of interpersonal communication as it might apply to adults or to children. The chapters on listening, for example, look at the importance of being an attentive listener, and how this can encourage communication in adults and children, and at factors which make communication difficult at any age, and how these can be avoided.

Overall the aims of the book are that the reader should:

- become more aware of the central place of interpersonal communication in their work;
- come to an understanding that effective interpersonal communication depends on skills that can be acquired;
- learn to communicate in ways which meet the needs of the children they work with.

Content of chapters

Chapter 1 is an introduction to the subject: it discusses interpersonal communication in general and looks particularly at verbal and non-verbal communication. Chapter 2 is about an interpersonal approach with babies and discusses a particular type of non-verbal communication: preverbal communication, that is, communication before the child acquires language. Chapters 3–6 are in a sequence and are about listening – a core skill for people who work with children. Chapter 7 looks at self-disclosure: communicating about oneself to children and others, when this is helpful in the work situation and when it is inappropriate. Chapter 8 focuses on different types of questions and their uses; it also examines the questions adults address to children as well as children's questioning of adults.

Chapter 9 looks at social control in interpersonal communication, including ways in which some groups of people are given a lower status than others. It examines equal opportunities in the context of interpersonal communication, with discussion and exercises on sexism, racism and people with disabilities in children's services. This chapter may be read out of sequence.

Chapters 10 and 11 present ways of communicating in a constructive manner in situations where there is conflict, including how to approach children or adults about behaviour which is unacceptable and how to receive criticism. This draws heavily on what has been learned in Chapters 3–6 and may be read immediately after these chapters.

Chapter 12 is entirely new and gives advice about working in groups and meetings. It can be applied to staff meetings and parents' groups, or meetings for children. It looks at being an effective group member and at setting up and leading a group. Again, this chapter draws on much that has been learned earlier in the book.

Chapter 13 takes up the subject of confidentiality in early years and play work. It not only stresses the importance of not divulging personal information about children and their families, but also looks at when it is essential to let senior staff know about any serious concerns there may be about a child.

Chapter 14 draws together all the main themes of the book.

Exercises and observations

Communicating with Children and Adults contains many exercises, including suggestions for observations and materials for discussion. The discussion material is headed 'Points to discuss or think about', and is useful for the student working on his or her own, or not taking part in a course, who can still take time to reflect on the case studies that are presented and the questions that are posed. Where the book is being used on a course, discussion can take place in small groups or the whole class can take part together. Some tutors may wish to use the discussion points as the basis for written work.

Any exercises or observations in the students' workplace or elsewhere can be usefully discussed at the next session by all those who have done the exercise. Comparing experiences can lead to further understanding of what aids effective communication and what hinders it.

Carrying out observations

There are many suggestions for observations in this book. Some are for carrying out observations at the workplace or on training placement. Others are for observations to carry out at home or elsewhere. In some chapters it is suggested that the student watches television for the purpose of observing interpersonal communication. It would be possible for a class tutor to record short excerpts from a television drama for observation and discussion by the whole class.

Observing is a useful way of learning about behaviour, including how people communicate together.

Carrying out an observation is not the same as just casually watching what is happening: it means watching in such a way that you learn all you can from a situation.

There are two main types of suggestions for observation made in the book: formal and less formal. A more formal observation is one in which you make an arrangement to carry out the observation, for example, in a play centre, a nursery or with a mother and child, and then carry it out, over a set period of time, at the same time making a written record of your observations.

Formal observations

If you are observing interpersonal communication formally, there are certain steps to be taken in advance. It is essential to obtain permission to carry out the observation at a time which is convenient for the people who will be involved.

From the outset be very clear about the sort of communication on which you will concentrate. Before you start, copy out the aim of the observation (suggestions are included throughout the book) and what you are going to look out for. Take with you two pens or pencils (in case one fails), writing paper, a clipboard and a watch to time the observation.

Explain to any adults who are present that you are doing an observation as part of your training. Ask if any of the children are going to be removed from the room for any purpose during the observation period. Do not include these as 'target' children (see below) in the observation.

It is sometimes a good idea just to watch for ten minutes, before you start to observe properly. During this time if any children approach you and try to get you talking or show you things, tell them in a friendly way that today you cannot talk because you are going to be busy writing. They will soon understand and leave you free to observe.

To begin with, you can make some notes describing the background to the observation: for example, the sort of room you are in, how many children are present, their age range, the number of staff present and whatever activities are going on. This gives a context for your observation.

If the observation is to be of several children, observe each one for several minutes. The child under observation is known as the 'target child'. Do not let your attention wander from one child to another.

Make notes about each episode of communication as it happens, then return to observing.

Devise your own shorthand for your notes, in advance. For example, call the child you are observing X (and other children who approach the observation child A, B, C). Identify any adults involved by a number: $1, 2, 3$. Use *pl* for play, *gv* for gives, *t* for touches, *sm* for smiles, and so on. Do not have too many abbreviations or you will forget them. Write down a short list of those you are going to use in advance.

Try to be as factual as you can in your observation. Say what is happening and do not give your opinion about it; so write: 'The baby is crying', not 'The baby is making a terrible noise'.

This style of carrying out observations can also be used when observing characters in television programmes (some exercises suggest observing interpersonal communication on television). You will have to be ready, in this case, to switch attention from one character to another if there is a change of scene, as you will not know about it in advance.

If you have the opportunity, carry out the same observation exercise more than once. This gives you useful practice.

Less formal observations

Some of the suggestions in this book are for less formal observations; for example, observations in a public place, such as a station or park playground. On these, and other occasions, it could be difficult to write down your observations there and then. In such a case you should write notes about what you noticed and anything that you learned as soon as possible after the event. You can write them more fully later.

Elsewhere it is suggested that you be aware of certain types of communication as they happen around you, in the nursery or in everyday life: for example, the use of questions or how adults respond to children. Clearly, it is not possible to write notes about unplanned episodes in the same way as formal observations. In many circumstances, it would not be acceptable to take out a pen and make notes, there and then. Nevertheless, it is useful to write a description of the people involved, how the interaction progressed and any outcome that you were aware of. The important thing is to become alert to how people communicate.

Confidentiality

It is very important that individuals should not be identifiable from any-thing you write as a result of your observations. Do not use any names in case a third party comes across your notes and can identify the people con-cerned. This includes children's names and adults' names and the name of any nursery, school, playscheme or other service.

1 Interpersonal communication

Throughout this book it is taken for granted that readers will wish to communicate effectively with all the people with whom they come into contact: babies, children, parents, colleagues and others. This chapter explains what is meant by interpersonal communication and introduces some of the ways in which people communicate *in person*. Communicating effectively face to face is an activity which is satisfying, interesting and sometimes very demanding. It is the central process in working with children in early years and play work and is first and foremost *personal*. The book does not cover written communication, important as this may be in passing on information, or requests to parents, or members of staff. Letters, notices and posters do not involve a direct interpersonal encounter between people and so are outside the scope of this book.

Interpersonal communication takes place when people – adults and children – interact. They talk, listen, observe and react to each other, exchanging all kinds of information, in many different ways. They are present to each other. Communication is the very stuff of social life. From babyhood onwards, we inform other people about ourselves, our needs, feelings and ideas. The content of our communication is as varied as life itself, from our angry cries as frustrated toddlers to the words of encouragement we give to the children we work with. Similarly, other people, whether they are children or adults, communicate their experiences, their feelings and their knowledge to us.

A useful way of thinking about interpersonal communication is as a series of messages – information – which you send out to other people and messages which you receive from them, through seeing, hearing or touching one another. So a toddler who points insistently towards a dog and says 'daw ... daw ...' is sending you a message about something that has caught her attention. She may look towards you to check that you see what she sees. If you receive her message you may give her an answering message – a smile, a nod or some words: 'Yes, it's a dog.'

A ten year old taps on your arm to get your attention and, without a word, but with great delight, holds up a completed model, the paint still wet, for your attention. The message may be complex: perhaps pride in achievement and confidence that you will understand and share that pride.

As a human being, you make use of sophisticated equipment in order to communicate, both to send and to receive information. You use your face, body and voice for sending messages to other people and your senses –

Messages pass from one person to another through touch, sounds, gestures and expressions as well as words

sight, hearing and touch – for receiving them. These are backed up by your brain and, equally importantly, by all your experience of human communication, so that you can make sense of incoming messages and co-ordinate outgoing ones.

But this is not the whole story. Remember that communication is an exchange and there are always at least two people engaged in it. Imagine someone reciting a speech alone in the bathroom or a child smiling in a hiding place where no one can see her; however inspiring the words or expressive the smile, these two people are not communicating – because no one is listening to the orator in the bathroom and no one observes that the child is happy.

In the past a popular saying in nursery work was 'bathe the child with language' (and certainly it is necessary for children to hear language in order to speak and understand), but flooding children with language is not the same as communicating effectively with them. If they do not understand, or do not want to listen, the message you are trying to communicate is blocked. Similarly, there is more to communicating with the adults you meet at work than simply telling them something. Unless they take part by listening to you, there is no communication or what you intended to convey can be distorted. Communication takes place when someone sends a message and the other person receives it. It is a two-way process.

You play your part in communication by listening to and observing other people when they are communicating with you, as well as by talking to them. Listening carefully to the other person, and being sensitive to their feelings and to their point of view, is a way of respecting them and being open to their communications.

Observation

- Spend half an hour observing interpersonal communication in a place where adults and children are together; for example, it could be a nursery, a kids' club, a park sandpit or a playground. Become aware of who starts any communication between adults and children – the adult or the child?
- Notice how many ways people can communicate, other than with words. Do the communications seem to be successful – do people get through to one another – or not?
- What discoveries did you make?

Non-verbal communication

After carrying out the observation just outlined, you may have become more aware of the means of communication that children and adults use. Verbal communication is important, but there are other ways of letting people know what we think and what we feel which are used even more frequently than words. These ways are called non-verbal communication.

People convey messages non-verbally by using:

- their voices,
- their faces,
- their bodies.

Voices communicate

The way that people speak has an effect on the meaning of the words they use. Experiment saying the phrase, 'Would you like to go swimming?' to convey different messages to the other person, for example:

'I like doing things with you ...'
'I feel bored ...'
'I don't think you heard me the first time ...'
'I'm in a hurry ...'

You will find that the same words can carry very different meanings according to how someone uses their voice.

Become aware of some of the following when you are listening to people:

- the speed at which they speak: fast, slow, speeding up, slowing down;
- how they pause or hesitate in what they say;
- the volume: loud, shouting, moderate, very quiet, whispering, inaudible;
- the pitch of the voice: high, screeching, low, middle register;
- inflection: how the voice rises and falls;
- the emphasis or stress they give to certain words.

MEANINGFUL SOUNDS

People of all ages make wordless sounds to convey messages to other people. These include sighs, squeals, laughs, moans, yawns and cries. You may have noticed that children are less inhibited than adults in using their voices like this! Imagine a moment of great excitement in an adventure playground, or of conflict between toddlers in a day nursery.

BEING SENSITIVE TO VOICES

A member of staff who is sensitive to how people use their voices is in touch with a great deal of information about how children and colleagues are feeling. For example, you know just by a change in the quality of her squeals of laughter that a baby is no longer happily excited with a rough-and-tumble game but is on the verge of becoming anxious. So you quieten the game down and reassure her.

You may be talking to a parent who replies quietly, slowly and hesitantly, using little emphasis. You realize that she sounds depressed, and you take this into account in how you respond to her. This is probably not the right moment to overload her with information about a minor matter concerning her child.

Observation

- Watch a play or 'soap' on television for 15 minutes paying special attention to one main character and how that person uses their voice. Notice the speed, pauses, volume, pitch and inflection with which the person speaks.
- What is communicated to other people through the way the actor uses their voice?

Faces communicate

Whether we intend it or not, faces can convey a great deal of meaning. Some people control their expressions and look disconcertingly 'dead pan'. Others have very mobile faces, showing fleeting thoughts and emotions clearly. The following photographs show something of the range of expressions you might come across at work, whether on the faces of staff, volunteers, parents or children. What do you think the various expressions mean? Is it easy to interpret them?

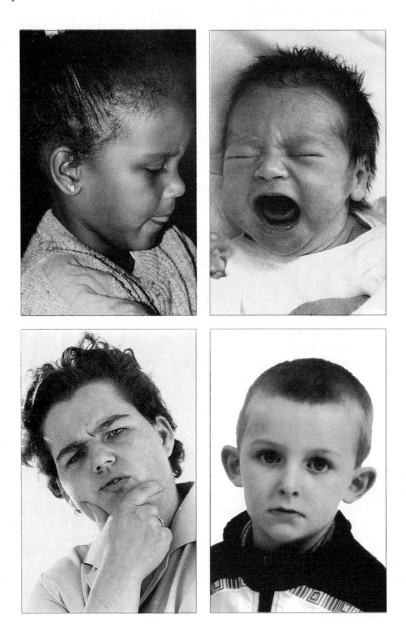

Faces convey much information about how people are feeling

Smiling, gazing and frowning are all common and important ways of communicating by making use of the face.

- *Smiling* needs no explanation. It is something we have all done from the time we were a few months old and the messages communicated by a smile are for the most part clear: 'I'm happy ... pleased ... friendly ...' These are positive, warm messages. We also recognize an insincere smile when we see it. This comes from the head rather than the heart, and involves the mouth but – chillingly – not the eyes.

- *Gazing* means looking directly into the face of another person, perhaps gazing into their eyes. People gaze unselfconsciously; for example, you usually look towards someone who is speaking if you are interested in what they have to say – turning your gaze away may put them off.

  In the next chapter we shall see that in interactions with babies, their gazing into your eyes and their smiles play a significant part in your communications together.

- When someone draws their brows together in a *frown*, it can show that they are puzzled, anxious or displeased. It can be easy to conclude, at first glance, that someone is displeased, when they are in fact frowning because of anxiety. So take all the circumstances into account before jumping to conclusions about frowns. Is a father resentful about what you have said about his child, or could it be that you have raised anxieties for him?

Observation

Watch a television play or 'soap' for 15 minutes but turn the sound off. Concentrate on how the actors use their faces. How easy is it to follow the story without words? Do different characters seem to have a different range of expressions? Which facial expressions give the clearest messages?

Bodies communicate

Many messages are conveyed by the way we use our bodies. We touch, turn away, face someone, stand close or move apart, and make body movements and gesticulations. All of these are components of body language.

TOUCH

The most direct messages are those conveyed by touch. In different countries people use touch to varying extents. In Britain, for example, communicating through touch, except for the conventional handshake, is usually reserved for people who have a close relationship. However, in certain types of professional work, such as hairdressing or medicine, staff are 'allowed' to touch people with whom they have no close personal relationship. There are also occasions where touch cannot be avoided, such as during the rush hour on crowded public transport, when strangers do not treat contact with others as a form of personal communication. In other cultures, for example among Arab people, touch plays a much bigger part in daily communications between people who do not have a close relationship.

Even within a society where using touch is less common, different people have their own style. Some happily put an arm round a friend's shoulder, or give delighted hugs to communicate their pleasure. Other, less demonstrative, people rely more on words or smiles to convey their feelings.

In your interactions with children, especially younger children, touch can be an important element of communication. For nursery workers, the sheer bodily care of children as you change, wash, dress and feed them requires contact and closeness. How you carry out this physical care conveys to the child how you feel about them, and what may seem like routine tasks for you need not be so for the child. These are times when your attention is on one child rather than a group, so this is an ideal time for talking to them and getting to know them. But you need to feel unhurried and to bring to routine care tasks the understanding that they provide you with unique opportunities for communication which you can both enjoy.

You can talk about what you are doing, take time to answer questions, sing songs and play games. Dressing a child can be just the time for playing finger games, or counting on their toes or playing knee-riding games such as, 'This is the way the ladies ride'. Over and above the touches involved in physical care, physical contact is a necessary feature in play and communicating, especially with babies and toddlers. Stroking, hugging, cuddling, holding, bouncing and swinging can all convey important messages to the young children you work with: they tell them in a very direct way that you accept them, feel warm towards them and enjoy their company.

Unfortunately, the opposite can also be true: touching can pass on many varied messages. It can be playful, gentle, firm, careless or harsh. It can say, 'I like you', or 'You are a nuisance and I wish this was over', or 'I am confident and you are safe in my hands'. Children are aware of their caregivers' feelings towards them, which is why liking children and enjoying their company is an essential qualification for working with them.

Points to discuss or think about

Janey likes her work, but there is a new toddler in her group who really seems to 'get under her skin'. He does not seem to cooperate when she dresses him and he hangs his head when she approaches. She is becoming more aware of this as the weeks go by. What should she do?

UNWANTED TOUCHES

Since the late 1980s there has been a growing awareness of child sexual abuse. This is more often carried out by adults known to children, such as members of the family and friends, rather than by strangers.* Cases involving nursery or play staff are very rare. Nevertheless, managers of nurseries and play provision must be sensitive to the possibility, however remote, and take steps to reduce any risk. Procedures include carrying out police checks for any record of conviction (although this is not a legal obligation for provision in the private and voluntary sector), asking staff to declare any criminal record, scrutinizing work histories for unexplained gaps, and taking up references. The on-going support and supervision of staff and volunteers also provides an important safeguard. Ideally, all children's services should have a clear policy about physical contact between adults and children and this should be communicated to, and discussed with, staff and volunteers.

All this is necessary, but it would be unfortunate if such precautions were to make staff self-conscious in their relationships with children and uneasy about ever touching them. A touch, whether an arm round the shoulder or a hug, may be the most appropriate way of responding to a child who is in distress or who is enormously happy. Staff need to trust themselves and their own responses in these circumstances.

In general, as children develop from babies and toddlers, through their early school years and into adolescence, casual, friendly touching between children and adults outside the family decreases and becomes less appropriate. In the end it is at about the same level as it is between adults. Workers who are sensitive to children are, perhaps without realizing it, sensitive to whether or not children accept or reject physical contact. Children – even

*See for example *Child Sexual Abuse* (1992). The Children's Legal Centre: London.

quite young ones – do not always welcome being touched by people who are not familiar to them. This should always be respected. Perhaps you can remember being reluctant to kiss a relative whom you hardly knew?

If children are treated as individuals who have their own rights, including the right to be heard on any matter that concerns them, they may also come to understand that they have the right to say 'no' to any unwanted touches. This includes being touched by other children. It is also important that they feel free to tell a responsible adult about anything which causes them unease. For this to happen children must be consistently listened to and respected as partners in communication, rather than as merely subordinate to the adult members of staff. Listening to children is an important theme of this book, which is treated in detail in later chapters.

It may be that a child or adolescent touches an adult worker in a way that the worker finds too intimate and unacceptable. If this happens, the worker should make it clear that the behaviour is not appropriate. How this is done depends on the age of the child. A simple movement, such as removing a hand, might be enough; or the worker might need to give a clear verbal message that the behaviour is not acceptable (see pages 99–100 on 'boundary-setting'). Except in the case of incidents involving babies or very young children, it would often be appropriate to mention what had happened to a senior worker.

Other 'body language'

As well as through touch, there are three other important ways to communicate through body language.

THE ORIENTATION OF THE BODY

This means the extent to which you face someone or turn away from them during communication: whether you are alongside someone and looking in the same direction; whether you are facing them head on; whether you talk to them over your shoulder; or whether you turn your back on them, not looking at them at all. Bodily orientation gives its own messages.

Imagine a playscheme worker putting out a snack for the children. A small boy comes up and pulls at his trouser leg. The worker speaks to the child over his shoulder, without turning to face him. This gives the message that the worker is not willing, at that moment, to give full attention to the child.

You can also receive information from other people's orientation towards you. A child who has been given a nursery place in an emergency, without any time for his parents to settle him in, turns away and hangs his head when you approach him. You realize that he is still feeling strange and needs tactful attention.

CLOSE OR DISTANT

The distance that people maintain between each other, and any changes in that distance, can be significant messages about their feelings. In some societies, adults usually stand or sit quite close to one another. In others, they 'keep their distance' unless they are with friends or relations. They can feel quite threatened if someone else comes too close. But when an adult and a child are communicating, they often come very close when they know one another well.

BODY MOVEMENTS AND GESTURES

These can convey meaning. There are many different kinds and they include such different gestures as waving a hand, shaking a fist, fidgeting with boredom or discomfort, and tapping the foot in annoyance. Some of these gestures are conscious, such as waving or pointing, but sometimes people do not realize that their movements give messages. For example a mother may smile when you say you are sorry for keeping her waiting and say 'It's quite all right, I'm not in a hurry', but give away her true feeling by tapping her foot.

At this point a word of caution is necessary. It is not always easy to interpret non-verbal communication and you always need to take into account other aspects of what is happening before jumping to conclusions about what any particular piece of 'body language' may mean. In the last example, if the mother was tapping her foot in time to music on the radio, the movement would have quite a different meaning from a situation where a car was waiting to take her home.

Observation

Spend a quarter of an hour in a public place, such as a station, park or shopping centre, and notice the ways in which people use their bodies to communicate.

- Observe facial expressions; watch their hands and feet.
- How close are people to each other?
- Do they touch?
- What is their orientation to each other?

What do you learn about the relationships between people from their body language? What feelings do they express?

Points to discuss or think about

- Why is knowing about interpersonal communication useful for nursery workers?
- In a summer playscheme, where the provider was very conscious of child abuse issues, staff were told that, for their own sakes, they must never touch a child unless they knew the reason for doing so in advance, for example, to comfort a child, to help them to use a swing, or to deal with an injury. This was so that they might have an explanation in case a child or parent later made accusations against them.

  This approach is not followed by staff in another scheme. They often hug children, kiss them or take them on their knee, whether to comfort them or as an expression of affection. They see their relationship with the children as a personal one, which includes a certain amount of intimacy.

  What are the advantages and disadvantages of these two different approaches?

INTERPERSONAL COMMUNICATION: KEY POINTS

- Interpersonal communication takes place when people – adults, children and babies – are together and messages are sent backwards and forwards between them.
- The messages can be about ideas, feelings, facts or a mixture of these. A question is also a message, a request for information.
- The two main forms of interpersonal communication are verbal and non-verbal.
- Verbal communication is communication based on spoken words.
- Non-verbal communication consists of messages from one person to another conveyed by means other than words (although they can accompany words).
- Non-verbal communication includes the way people use their voices, facial expressions and bodies to convey meaning.

2 Preverbal communication

This chapter is especially for people who work with babies, because babies can also take part in communication. They cannot of course use words or, to begin with, understand them. Nevertheless, they have other ways of interacting with people. Communication at this stage of life is known as *preverbal* because it takes place before a child can talk.

From the beginning, babies seem to be designed to communicate with those who care for them – they are very sociable beings. This makes working with babies much easier. As you carry out such routine tasks as feeding, changing and bathing and when you play with them it is not difficult to find yourself responding to babies, as well as taking the initiative. Together with their parents you will be playing your part in accompanying them into the rich experiences of human communication. While babies are born with great potential for communication, they learn to communicate through their interactions with you and with their other caregivers. An obvious example is that they learn words and the use of words because you and other people talk to them.

Their potential for communication will increase alongside their growing experience and intellectual development as the years go by. As a nursery worker you can play an important part in their progress by becoming more effective as communicators.

What babies lack as communicators

In order to be an effective communicator, a person needs to be in control of their communication and to *intend* to communicate. Young babies do not have intentions in the way we usually understand the word; they do not think things over or make plans about what they are going to do or how they are going to do it.

In order to communicate effectively a person needs to have the necessary means – like language or gesture – for passing on their intended message. Babies have yet to learn the words and gestures used to convey meaning.

In order to communicate effectively people must be able to understand the other person's point of view so that they can get their message across. Good communicators try to make sure they are properly understood; for example, they speak more distinctly to people with hearing loss and choose simpler words when they talk to children. (Even a small child will do this, speaking more simply to a younger brother or sister.) Because their under-standing is very limited, it is months before babies realize that other people have a separate existence from themselves so the ability to see things from another's point of view develops slowly – although there are signs that this is beginning during the second year.

Babies and preverbal communication

From birth, babies are already equipped for the experiences which pave the way for communication.

- Babies find you and the other people who look after them fascinating. They are drawn to look at your face and its movements. It has just the sort of simple pattern and contrasts of light and dark that capture their atten-tion. Eyes, because they sparkle and move, are particularly fascinating.
- Babies are held by the sound of the human voice, especially when it is used in the special way that people have for talking to babies (see page 22).

But it is not just that babies are attracted by your face and voice. Babies play their part in drawing you into communication with them, getting your attention and causing you to linger, play and talk. Babies soon learn that their actions bring about results and that they have an effect on other people. In the early months you are their most irresistible plaything: interesting and novel yet somewhat controllable.

Throughout the animal kingdom the characteristics and behaviour of young animals have a predictable effect on adult members of a species, which helps the species to survive. Think how a mother bird is impelled to pop food into the open beak of a nestling. For human beings there seem to be similar processes at work. Let us look at some examples of non-verbal, in fact preverbal, ways in which babies capture and hold your attention and how they respond to you.

Appearance

For many people a baby's appearance – the large eyes and forehead, tiny nose and, later, toddling walk – brings about a feeling of tenderness and a wish to protect. It is one of the signals which results in babies being looked after and responded to and which draws adults into communication with them.

Crying

For newborn babies a significant lesson is that when they cry someone turns up with comfort, food or attention. They are beginning to gain some control over their environment. Babies who are continually left to cry miss out on an important piece of learning.

Looking into your eyes

Your face, and especially your eyes, are fascinating for young babies. They hold your gaze with their own in a way that can be irresistible and leads you on to talk and play. Similarly, when they have had enough, or want a few seconds rest, you will notice that they turn their eyes away until they are ready for more interaction. Adults who are sensitive to the baby's signals do not try to prolong games or conversations for longer than the baby wishes.

Smiling

At around two or three months, babies find a new and delightful way of attracting attention and engaging you in interaction – their first real sociable smiles when they look into your eyes. (You may notice even earlier smiles, but these are often in response to sensations in the digestive system, 'windy smiles'.) Adults find babies' smiles very rewarding and often work quite hard to get the baby to produce one.

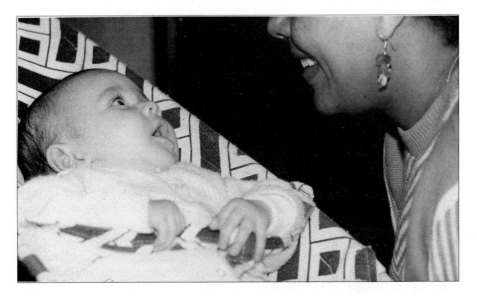

Babies have their own ways of interacting with people

Laughing

Some weeks after the first smile comes laughter. A baby's laugh can immediately draw you into play – to the great enjoyment of you both. Other signs of pleasure are the wriggles and squeals of delight when you approach and the special moment when a baby first holds out both arms to be lifted up.

Sounds

To start with, the baby makes sounds that are rather haphazard and not very distinctive. Then, at about four or five months, they start to make a cooing 'agoo' and like you to join in, saying the sound back, taking a turn in the conversation. This is a sound that you can get babies of just this age to repeat after you, once they can produce it spontaneously themselves. They also develop a more boisterous selection of sounds: spluttering, blowing raspberries and producing quite earsplitting noises inviting you to join in the fun.

Look out for how they use lips and tongue in small movements, pushing the tongue out between the teeth, bringing the lips together and then breathing out with a little bubble of saliva. These early movements, coordinating breath with the articulation of tongue and lips, are part of the baby's early attempts at producing speech.

Towards seven months, babies produce sounds which are more like those found in adult speech. They produce consonants using the lips – like 'b' – and using the tongue – like 'd'. Also syllables such as 'ba' and 'da' make an appearance – all steps along the road to speech, which will develop very rapidly in the next year.

Babble and 'talk'

The syllables develop into endless repetitions – ba-ba, da-da-da-da-da – for the pleasure of hearing the sounds and the sensations they produce in the baby's mouth. Infants in most cultures, whatever language is spoken around them, make similar sounds at this stage and make them in the same sequence. However, by the time they have gone through this basic sequence, certainly by one year old, babies are moving towards whichever language they are accustomed to hearing. They now produce the sounds and intonation patterns of the language spoken by the people around them and spend a lot of time pretending to talk, having conversations with themselves and with anyone else who wants to join in.

These are pretend conversations in which you can play your part, absorbed in the baby's contribution, imitating, pretending to understand, answering either in your own adult language or with sounds similar to the baby's own. It may sound like fun – and it is – but it is also a way of leading the baby further into the world of communication.

Nursery rituals and recognition

Before they reach their first birthday babies enjoy the games and rituals you build up together and recognize them as they fit into the nursery day. They remember the various signs that things are going to happen: the rattle of pans at dinner time, coats and scarves mean it is time to go out. They are now sensitive to your facial expressions and can see when you are pleased and when you are cross. Words are also starting to carry meaning. At about eight months they understand 'No' and (may!) respond accordingly. Also, around this age some babies recognize their names and look round when called.

Letting you know how they feel

Towards the end of the first year crying and smiling are still powerful signals, but babies now have other ways of attracting your attention and letting you know what they want. They reach out for things beyond their grasp, pull at your trouser leg or at your skirt to get you to notice, and shake their heads vigorously or scuttle off in the opposite direction if they do not want to cooperate.

Imitation

By about ten months old babies imitate your actions and those of other adults who hold an important place in their lives. They play peep-bo, clap hands and cooperate in games of pat-a-cake; they remember and use social gestures, such as waving 'Bye-bye' and blowing kisses.

These are just some of the ways in which babies respond to you and get you to communicate with them. But as well as supplying their own part they are continually learning from you. By the time the baby is a year old, interacting with you and with other adults has played a major part in the baby's developing potential as a communicator.

Observation

Spend some time observing a baby interacting with an adult. You might visit a local child welfare clinic, a mothers' or childminders' drop-in centre, a nursery – or arrange to observe a parent and baby at home.

Describe the part played by the baby in each episode of interaction – which may be short or prolonged.

Include the following: does the baby seem to involve the adult in any interactions? How does this happen – what does the baby do? How does the baby respond to the adult? Who seems to finish each interaction, the adult or the baby?

Adults and preverbal communication

If you watch someone who enjoys working with babies you will notice that they behave as though the baby is a fully communicating person and already understands every word that is said. They treat babies as partners in communication and encourage them to take their turn in 'conversations' and play; they listen to what the baby has to 'say'; they ask plenty of questions such as, 'You like it, don't you?' and: 'It's nice and warm, isn't it?', speaking in a special tone of voice, used just for babies, repeating themselves for the baby's benefit: 'Yes it's nice and warm.' They speak quite slowly and distinctly, sometimes with exaggerated changes of pitch and emphasis. They wait for the baby's reply, and if it is not forthcoming they supply it themselves. 'Mm, I like that. That's nice.' This special way of talking to babies has been called 'mothereze', because it seems to come naturally to many mothers. Meanwhile the baby gazes into the adult's face, watching and listening attentively, and taking their turn with movements, smiles and sounds.

Sensitive adults are attentive to all the information they receive from the baby. They time their actions, movements and words to synchronize, fit in, with the actions of the baby. For example, during feeds they allow themselves to be paced by the baby: they wait to speak, or to rock the baby gently, during the short intervals when the baby is not actually sucking. They are quiet when the baby starts to feed again. In fact, they let the baby set the pace, gently responding to the noises made as though they were words.

Turn-taking

In this way, from the earliest days, babies are introduced to an important aspect of interpersonal communication: that we take turns, each listening while the other speaks or plays their part. Later in the book we shall return to turn-taking in adult conversations (see page 64).

Observation

Observe an adult and baby and this time pay special attention to the part played by the adult. How does the adult talk to the baby? Do you notice any 'turn-taking'?

Being sensitive to the baby's 'state'

People who are good at communicating are able to judge from various signals how the other person is feeling and to take this into account when they are communicating with them. As a nursery worker it is important when you are communicating with babies to be sensitive to their state of consciousness. This means how ready the baby is for communication and activity at any particular time. A baby's day has its own rhythm; at different times during the day the child goes from one state of consciousness to another. They pass from being deeply asleep, when it seems that nothing could disturb them, to a state of light sleep, fidgeting and easily disturbed. They can pass from this to a state of wakefulness – fully alert and observant, but quite still. They may then enter a phase of activity and movement. This in turn can be followed by fussing and then by full-blown crying. They may then return to one of the previous states, including drowsiness and sleep.

A newborn baby spends most of the time asleep. Nevertheless, there are many points during the day – often just after a feed – when a young baby is quiet, alert and ready for 'communication'. It is important to take advantage of these times and not just put the baby straight back to sleep. These are the best times for conversation and play, if only for a few minutes.

As the baby grows, such times become more frequent and longer. When babies are restless it could be that they are tired and will soon sleep. But you may find that you can bring them to a state of quiet attention – the state in which they are most able to take in what is happening – by talking, stroking, rocking them or showing them something interesting.

When they are crying, on the other hand, there is so much interference (see pages 29–30) from noise, movement and discomfort that they are not able to attend to anything else. At these times it is better to soothe a baby rather than to attempt any more playful communications.

Observation

Observe a baby, whether with an adult or alone, for 20 minutes. Describe the 'state' that they are in and any changes in it over the observation period. Notice the following:

- How much movement is there? Observe the baby's arms, legs, trunk, head.
- What sounds does the baby make?
- Are they interested in what is happening around them?
- How absorbed is the baby in any activity, for example, a feed, a game or conversation?
- If the baby is asleep, how would you describe the sleep? Is it light, restless or deep? What is the baby doing that leads you to this judgement?
- Is anything responsible for bringing about a change from one state to another during the course of the observation?

Bilingual babies and children

Nursery workers may work with babies and children who are brought up bilingually. This is the case when the main language of one parent is different from that of the other, or when the child is looked after for part of the day by someone whose language is different from that spoken at home. Children with such bilingual backgrounds tend to acquire their languages more slowly than those who speak only one. However, research shows that they catch up with other children and later in childhood are at least as advanced in intelligence as others. They also have the advantage of being fluent in two languages.

Communication can be made easier for a baby who is exposed to two languages. Whoever is involved in looking after the baby should speak consistently to the child in one language only. So the nursery workers should speak one language consistently, while the parents should always use the other. In this way the baby comes to associate the different languages with the people who speak them – and is mentally prepared to hear what they have to say. Later they use whichever language is appropriate for the other person.

Points to discuss or think about

'You have to be really skilled to work well with babies.'
'Looking after babies comes naturally.'
'Babies are not as interesting as older children.'

- What do you think of these different points of view?
- What answers would you give, making use of what you have read in this chapter?

PREVERBAL COMMUNICATION: KEY POINTS

- Preverbal communication is communication in which one of the people involved has not yet developed language, for example, communication between an adult and a baby.
- Babies have great potential as communicators and can, if you let them, draw you into 'conversation' and play.
- Communicating with babies includes talking to them, touching them and playing with them. Communication is very important for a baby's well-being and development.
- People who enjoy looking after babies talk to them as though they understand. They use a special style of talking which attracts and holds the baby's attention; they time their contributions so that they fit in with those of the baby; they 'take turns' with the baby.
- Babies are most ready for talk and play when they are wakeful and alert. In this state they are better able to take things in than when they are fussing or sleepy.
- Babies who are brought up bilingually are at an advantage. It helps their acquisition of both languages if those who mainly interact with the baby keep to the same language; for example the mother always speaks English while the father always speaks Punjabi.

3 Careful listening

Whether it involves children, babies or adults, interpersonal communication is a two-way process. In communication it is useful to think of a person sending a message and someone receiving it. If no messages pass backwards and forwards, then communication does not take place. So, while talking has its part to play, listening (and observing) are also essential. In other words, it is vital for you to be able to listen carefully, to take in the information other people give you. Think of the occasions when you need to listen, and to listen carefully, in early years and play work.

- Throughout the day children have much to tell you about. They confide problems, explain games, ask for help, pass on jokes.
- Parents tell you important details about their children – about sleep patterns, their likes and dislikes at meal times and information about the child's health.

Listening is as important as talking

- Parents or staff speak about changes in a child's family and household arrangements.
- Parents may confide in you about their personal problems.
- Colleagues pass on details to do with the organization of your work, such as any changes caused by other staff being absent.
- Other professional workers may ask you to follow a certain course of action in your work with a child: for example, a speech therapist may want you to help a child who has problems being understood.

All these people need to be listened to carefully for the following reasons:

- Careful listening means that you cooperate better with parents and with fellow workers because you understand 'messages' that are important for your work.
- There is a new awareness of the child's right to be heard on matters that concern them. It can be found in much legislation including the Children Act 1989 and the United Nations Convention on the Rights of the Child. Children should have the experience of being listened to from the beginning, as this builds up their self-esteem and their sense of being a person. As you listen attentively to what they say, you come to know them better and begin to see things from their point of view – and this is especially important in your work with children. In early years and play work, children need people who are responsive and sensitive to them.

  Listening to what children say is an excellent way of coming to understand them, of developing your relationship and encouraging them to communicate with you. It also presents them with a model of how to treat other people.
- When you listen carefully to someone, they realize that you are taking them and their experience seriously, that you treat what they have to say with respect.

Exercise

Find a partner and take turns to listen carefully to one another. You each have five minutes to say why you chose to work with children, about any previous experience you have had of being or working with children, and what age group you prefer to work with.

After one person has spoken, the listener repeats what they can remember, with as much detail as possible. The speaker does not interrupt, but when the listener has finished, the speaker tells the listener if anything has been left out or is inaccurate.

When you have each had a turn as speaker and as listener, share with one another how you found the exercise: for example, if you found it hard to listen carefully, or if you thought it was hard to talk.

Listening can be difficult!

While listening is very important in early years and play work, it is not always easy.

I would like to paint a picture of two imaginary situations. The first is something of a dream world and the second a nightmare.

Dream nursery

Here everyone listens carefully. The nursery worker just says, 'Will people please listen for a moment?', and all the children stop playing and look towards her; even Amira – who has just managed to get hold of the doctor's stethoscope which she has wanted all morning – becomes attentive; Wayne stops crying about his cut knee; the budgie in her cage stops chirping and swinging on her bell. Everyone is listening.

When parents come in the workers listen carefully to what they have to say; Cheryl, listening to a child's father, does not seem to notice two children pulling at her clothes for attention, nor that the twins are attacking one another with paint.

The parents also listen carefully to the nursery staff, even when they are in a hurry and are worried about getting to work on time.

And the staff are noted for the way they stop what they are doing – changing nappies, explaining how a video works to a four year old, adding up the dinner money – in order to pay attention to another worker.

Nightmare playscheme

This is a fairly typical day at nightmare playscheme. No one ever really listens to anyone else. A mother, who looks rather worried, is explaining to a play worker that her little boy has not slept well and is a bit off his food. She wondered whether to bring him today, but she felt she could not afford to miss work. All the time she is talking, the play worker is gazing out of the window, wondering if it is warm enough to fill the paddling pool.

The children do not listen to anyone; they all seem to live in little worlds of their own. They cannot get anyone else to play with them, because the other children just do not pay attention.

The parents are too anxious to listen to the staff properly. They think that the staff are often critical of them and so they are always on the defensive and do not take in necessary information the staff give them. When it is the day for swimming, few children are sent with costumes, even though staff often remind parents in person.

As for staff meetings, these are angry occasions where people talk but do not listen. There are lots of interruptions and voices are often raised. Strangely enough the louder the voices the less they are heard!

Shouting doesn't help people to listen

Points to discuss or think about

- Both of these impossible establishments are fictitious but they both point to one conclusion: listening is not always easy. What reasons can you find for this in the accounts of the two establishments given above?
- Think of your own examples of circumstances which make listening difficult – whether at work or in everyday life.

Listening and hearing are not the same

It is important to understand that listening and hearing are not the same. While I am writing I am hardly aware of the sounds around me but, when I stop and listen, I can hear a car outside in the street, somewhere a radio is playing and there are voices outside my door.

These sounds were there all the time but they were not claiming my attention. I was preoccupied with what I was writing and so was not getting strong messages from outside. It was almost as though I had taken a telephone off the hook and no calls were coming through.

Something similar can happen in conversation. In certain circumstances, although I can hear the other person perfectly well, what they are saying does not get through. It is as though the information they wish to pass on is sabotaged in some way. Either it is completely blocked, or something does not register or, in some cases, whatever gets through is distorted and muddled. Let me give you some early years and play work examples of what I mean:

- A play worker is getting out brightly coloured papers, paint and glue so that any children who want to can use them to make masks. He is quite excited about it because he went to a mask-making training course last week and can see endless possibilities. Suddenly he realizes that he cannot find a bag of tinsel left over from last year's Christmas tree. He rummages about in the bottom of his bag, but cannot find it. A boy comes in and says that he has had a rotten day at school. 'Did you?' the worker asks, automatically, 'Poor thing,' at the same time turning out the contents of the bag on to the floor and rapidly sorting through. He has not registered that the boy is really quite upset, because he is too preoccupied with finding the tinsel. The boy sees the play worker is not interested and wanders off.

- A childminder is asking a mother if she could bring in a new supply of disposable nappies. The mother, meanwhile, is watching engrossed as her baby reaches out for a rattle and, for the first time in her life, manages to grasp hold of it successfully. The next day, she does not bring the nappies. Although she 'heard' the childminder's voice (the sound waves caused her eardrum to vibrate and nerves carried impulses to the brain) she was not listening; the minder's words made no impression on her.

- A play worker is telling a mother over the telephone that her child has had a fit. The mother immediately feels anxious. The worker says that the child seems to be fine now and that the staff have given the child the medication which the mother had left in case this should happen. He explains the details of what happened and the severity and length of the fit. When she puts the phone down the mother finds it difficult to remember in any detail what he has told her.

- A mother is about to take her turn on a playgroup volunteers' rota for the first time. Her child has only attended for a few days. She is quite nervous and worries in case her child is 'naughty' or over-demanding. The worker talks to her and says that the best thing for her to do is to give as much attention to her own child as he seems to need and not to bother about anything else. 'He'll soon find his feet,' she says. But the mother does not seem to take in what the worker says. It does not fit her image of being a helper and she continues to feel guilty that she needs to give so much attention to her own child. As a result neither she nor the child is happy.

- An inexperienced nursery teacher looks at a child's drawing of two people. 'My nan has gone to the hospital with grandpa,' he says. The teacher is very concerned that the children should start to learn elementary mathematical ideas. 'Oh, yes,' she answers, looking at the picture, 'Which is the bigger one ... which is the smaller one?' She does not seem to have listened to what could have been an important message from the child.

Interference

It is just as necessary to listen carefully to children as it is to listen carefully to adults. High quality listening shows that you respect people, that you think their experience, the things they tell you about and the questions they ask, are important to you. It is also a way of encouraging them to communicate – no one likes to be ignored or constantly misunderstood. But as you have seen, people, whether they are children or adults, are not always successful in their communications. The messages do not get through for many reasons – somewhere there is *interference* which blocks the way, either completely or only letting some parts of a message through. Interference can come from the speaker (the person who is sending the information) or the listener (the receiver). Sometimes there may be interference in both together! When this happens there is little chance of communication.

Below are some sources of interference – reasons why people cannot receive the verbal messages that are sent to them.

Reasons for interference and how to help

IMPAIRMENT

Hearing

When an adult or a child has some hearing loss, then obviously listening is more difficult for them and you have to be especially careful when you talk to them. The person with hearing impairment needs to see your face and lip movements easily, and you should make an effort to speak more distinctly. For a deaf parent, you should write down any important information. If you work for a local authority there may be a teacher for the deaf, or another special needs worker, who can give you advice.

Some adventure playgrounds, which aim to integrate children with disabilities, may train workers to use British Sign Language (BSL) to use with hearing-impaired children. Just as deaf children learn to lip-read spoken language, hearing children can soon become familiar with signs in BSL.

Speech

There may be some speech defect or impairment. For example, a child may have a cleft palate or a stutter and you will have to be especially patient in order to understand and to respond. In such cases extra professional help is needed. A speech therapist may be working with a child and the family; if so, it is good for early years or play workers to understand the approach the therapist is taking so that they can cooperate.

NOT HAVING THE SAME LANGUAGE

If you understand a few words of another person's language, and they understand a little of yours, much can be done just by trying to communicate – persevering patiently and carefully, using plenty of gestures until you make sense to one another – and a challenge like this can be fun. On other occasions, where understanding is vital, it is necessary to use an interpreter. This could be another parent, or in some places a local authority adviser could help you to find an interpreter and offer help generally. It is good to keep a list of local people who can be called on to interpret when necessary and to translate written communications. This may be in a voluntary or a paid capacity.

CHILDREN STILL ACQUIRING LANGUAGE

A young child's language is still immature so that they do not understand adult speech properly and also have difficulties in being understood. As you come to know a child you soon get on to the same wavelength, you find ways of saying things so that they understand, and figure out what they are trying to communicate. Again this needs patience but it is an essential part of your work and you should spend as much time as you can getting to know new children and helping them to get used to you. Children need people who are sensitive and responsive towards them if they are to get on well and be happy. And you cannot be sensitive towards a child until you can understand their 'messages' – what their words, their gestures and their expressions mean.

Even more mature children, including over-fives, can have difficulty in understanding you, and vice versa. When you have not shared much experience together, either of you may refer to events or use expressions which leave the other perplexed, although older children can be very persistent in trying to make sense of what you say. There is also the problem that children's understanding is limited. If you see that a child is struggling to understand, to make sense of what you are saying, you have to make extra efforts and find new ways of explaining.

DISTRACTIONS

Distractions are all the claims on your attention that can stop you from listening. Here are some possibilities:

- discomfort, for example, when a stuffy room is used for a staff meeting;
- physical pain, such as a headache;
- interruptions, such as when a parent wants to talk and a child is trying to get your attention at the same time;
- emotions, for example, anger, anxiety or sadness, which block or distort incoming or outgoing messages;
- thinking about other matters – a problem at home or at work, or day dreaming about some pleasant event;
- noise, which makes concentration difficult.

Avoiding distractions

As someone who works with people you need to be aware of any potential distractions, whether for yourself or others. Once you are aware of them you can take steps to avoid potential distractions so that effective interpersonal communication is possible.

It's difficult to concentrate in certain situations

Sometimes you may decide that this is not the right time or place to listen to someone properly. You may need to explain to a fellow member of staff that at the moment things are a bit hectic and ask if they could tell you about the staff party later on.

At other times you may decide that it is very important to listen at that moment and not to put someone off. For example, a mother comes in who is obviously upset. She asks if she can have a word with you. In this case you explain to the child who wants you to come to look at the rabbits *now,* that you will do so as soon as you have spoken to the parent. If there is another member of staff present, you may choose to listen to the mother in another, quieter, room.

If you are aware of distractions within yourself, such as a headache, or feelings of anxiety or wanting to think about other things, then you need to remind yourself to listen as carefully as you can.

If, on the other hand, you sense that the other person is distracted in similar ways, then you will need to take great care with your communication. It may be a good idea to ask if the other person has got some immediate concern on their minds, that is preoccupying them. This gives them a chance to talk about it, however briefly, so that they can give you greater attention afterwards. Or you may need to repeat what you have to say and check that they understand. This is especially helpful if you have to pass on details that the other person might find alarming: for example, if you need to explain to a mother that her child has bumped his head and been taken to hospital for a check-up. Often the parent needs more explanation, perhaps repeating the same questions, and getting you to say, more than once, exactly what has happened. In such cases it is helpful to ask, 'Is there anything you would like me to go over about what happened?', and allow her enough time to check out what she still needs to know.

Children also need to be undistracted if they are to listen properly. You may be having an interesting, important conversation with young children when suddenly the window-cleaner appears at the window. If the competition is too strong, it is pointless trying to go on with your previous conversation. In any case what is actually happening before the children's eyes is much more fascinating for them. It can be a starting point for children's play, for many activities and for further interesting conversations. If your earlier conversation was really important, then you will just have to find another time for it, when the children are not distracted.

You can see if someone else, of whatever age, is paying attention to you. A listening baby is quiet, their limbs are still and their eyes hold your gaze in a look of concentration and expectancy. Looking at the person who is talking, and not interrupting or fidgeting, are sure signs of listening for people of all ages. If these signs are absent, you will know that the message may not be getting through.

What about 'clear speech'?

You may be surprised to have come so far in this book without coming across a statement that it is important to speak clearly in order to communicate well. I hope that by now you understand that this point of view is an over-simplification. Clear, careful speech is often necessary, but it is not always sufficient for getting your message across.

Someone who speaks clearly does not necessarily get their message across to another person more effectively than someone who does not. An early years worker, or play worker, who speaks totally distinctly, with perfect grammar, can still, on occasion, fail to communicate. To communicate effectively, a person must also take into account factors which are likely to be a source of interference and do what they can to avoid or eliminate them. You can imagine the effect of talking about the differences between 'high' and 'low' or 'round' and 'square' to a child who is upset and crying. However clear and simple the worker's explanation and however careful and correct their speech, the child would understand little. To take another example, you would be wasting your time giving clear instructions about revised play-centre hours to someone who understood little English. In neither case would it be sensible to protest, 'But I explained very clearly.' Clear explanations are not always enough.

There are even times when people do not need to speak at all clearly, or use good grammar, in order to be understood perfectly. This may be the case between close friends and relatives, people who are very familiar to one another. For them a few words and gestures, 'Did you get the ...' or 'I asked but ...' may convey all the meaning necessary.

People who have a less close relationship need to speak more clearly to one another, in order to be properly understood. In formal situations like work – including work involving children – people become more formal in their speech and take more care with what they say and how they say it.

Nursery staff should be more careful of their speech at work than would be necessary at home. And, as was suggested earlier, it is often especially important to take much more care in situations where there is likely to be interference (see pages 29–33). However, when you get to know children, informal speech may, in many circumstances, be appropriate.

Points to discuss or think about

- In your experience, what is the most common sort of interference that gets in the way of communication?
- Do you think people listen as carefully to children as they do to adults?
- Why is it important to listen to children?
- What would you reply to someone who said, 'Children are too young to know what's best for them, so why should I bother listening to them'?

Observation

- Become aware of sources of interference when you are listening or trying to listen.
- Does your attention wander when someone is talking to you? Make notes of any occasions when this happens as soon as possible after the event and say why you were finding listening difficult.
- Look out for instances when you feel sure that someone is not really listening – perhaps to you. How do you know? Make notes about what happened.

CAREFUL LISTENING: KEY POINTS

- In interpersonal communication listening and observing (receiving messages) are as important as speaking (an aspect of sending messages).
- Careful listening is essential when you work with people: children, parents and colleagues should be listened to carefully.
- Careful listening shows respect and helps to avoid muddles. Listening to children helps you to get to know them and can encourage them to communicate with you.
- Careful listening is not always easy and 'interference' can occur. Interference means that a message is blocked or distorted. Sometimes the interference comes from the person who sends the message and sometimes from the person who receives it.
- Sources of interference include: hearing and speech impairments, not understanding each other's language properly and distractions arising, for example, from discomfort, interruptions and strong emotions.
- When talking and listening to others, early years and play workers should be alert to the possibility of interference and do what they can to eliminate it. Effective communication takes place when messages get through clearly, without being blocked or distorted.

4. Being an encouraging listener

If you spend any time observing someone who works with children you will see them taking part in a variety of interpersonal communication, including giving and asking for advice and explanation, posing questions, making jokes, asking for help and listening. Chapter 3 showed how listening carefully is important for effective communication. In this chapter we turn to being an *encouraging listener*, the sort of listener who enables both adults and children to communicate to the best of their ability. We have already seen that you need to be aware of and, if possible, avoid interference. Encouraging listening is to go one step further by giving other people your full attention and – this is essential – letting them know they have your full attention.

Let us look at some encouraging listening in action:

- Sally is carrying out a safety inspection up on the platform of a play structure in an adventure playground. Ian climbs up beside her, sobbing, and saying that his brother has just attacked him. Sally sees that he is upset and decides that the first priority is to listen to Ian. She stops what she is doing and crouches down beside him – at his level she can give him much more attention than looking down on the top of his head. He can see and hear her better, as well. She gives him her complete concentration and listens to him without interrupting. As Ian realizes that she is truly listening, he calms down and his story becomes easier to understand.
- It is the end of the afternoon when Renata's mother asks if this is a good time to ask Jenny, the early years worker, about something. As it happens this is a convenient moment and so Jenny takes her out into the garden where it is fairly quiet. At first the mother is hesitant; her story is complicated, involving her ex-husband and problems that arise after Renata's fortnightly visits to see him. Renata seems disturbed and does not settle down to sleep easily; she is also having quite a few tantrums. Jenny listens quietly. She occasionally nods her head, smiles her assurance that she is listening and takes her part in the conversation by means of the odd word of encouragement 'I see ... yes ... mm.' She asks no questions and offers no advice or explanations. Renata's mother seems to find this enough, for the moment, becomes less hesitant and starts to communicate more clearly. At this point attentive, encouraging listening is what she needs most from Jenny.

This sort of listening is not easy to start with. You may find that you desperately want to interrupt with a question, or give your point of view, or offer some advice. These may become appropriate later. In the first instance, when someone is upset they are not helpful. They could move the subject away from what the other person is anxious to discuss, towards something which is much more what you want to talk about. In fact, anything other than encouraging listening could have the effect of shutting up someone who needs to talk.

Attentive, encouraging listening can help someone let what is worrying them come to the surface, while offering advice or asking too many questions could be frustrating.

For example, Michael is worried that his son, Sean, is not eating enough. At the back of his mind is the memory of his own younger brother who was always sickly and died in childhood. Yesterday evening, Sean ate practically nothing and he has had no breakfast today. Michael is beginning to feel that he cannot cope. He is a single parent and has infrequent contact with the rest of his family.

The nursery worker hardly gives Michael a chance to explain what is on his mind but rushes straight in with reassurances that the child is perfectly healthy, that children eat what they need to eat and that there is no need to worry. She tells him about other children who eat little but grow up strong and healthy. When Michael continues to express his worries the worker starts to ask questions: 'Is the child having too many snacks between meals?'

Michael is put off by both the information and questions but, nevertheless, answers to the best of his ability. He is not helped, however, and goes away still burdened with an anxiety he needed to share.

The next day he approaches another, more experienced, nursery worker with his worry. This time the worker can see that Michael is very anxious, so she quietly hears him out before she gets round to making some suggestions. He is very relieved that she is obviously really listening and he feels able to confide the story of his brother. It is a relief to get this out in the open. When she feels that he has said what is on his mind, she reassures him and offers him some suggestions. He goes away feeling less anxious and able to take up the worker's advice.

Use 'encouraging listening' when it is appropriate

It is essential to become aware of the times when you really need to give your full attention and encouragement to adults and children – rather than taking an equal part in the conversation – so that they can find it easy to talk. It is especially useful when the other person is very excited or upset or has a great deal they need to say. It can also encourage someone who is shy to say what is on their mind.

When you first attempt to listen in this way, encouraging the other person to speak rather than making your own contribution, you may feel that it is rather artificial. On the other hand, it may seem perfectly natural. The art is in using encouraging listening at the right time. Obviously, if the other person is eager to hear your point of view, or asks straightforwardly for advice, it is very frustrating for them if you do not take part in the conversation.

How to be an encouraging listener

Here are some ways to be a good, encouraging listener.

- Attend carefully to what the other person is saying – you may need to make a conscious effort to ignore distractions.
- Let them know that you are listening, using non-verbal communication. Remember to:
  - keep your body and your head turned towards them;
  - with children, get down to their level if necessary;
  - do not move away;
  - use nods and smiles (where appropriate), to encourage them to continue talking;
  - look at them while they are talking – do not let your gaze wander about as though you are thinking about other things.
- Let them know that you are listening, by using verbal communication – use encouraging words and sounds, such as 'yes', 'I see', 'mm'.

Sometimes you need to say very little, just enough to reassure the person that you are listening and that you want them to continue

- Wait until they have finished what they have to say – interruptions are often frustrating and may discourage nervous people from speaking. *Do not butt in!*
- Avoid questions (unless there is something you really do not understand), explanations or advice – at any rate for the time being.

On many occasions this sort of listening is more valuable than having a discussion about a problem. You show by your encouragement that you are interested, that the speaker is not boring you and that you are putting their needs first. It is just a case of giving someone space to talk over whatever is on their mind. This helps them to think things through and often they can come up with their own solutions.

Points to discuss or think about

- What is most difficult about being a good listener?
- Have you ever been in a position where you would really have liked someone to listen wholeheartedly to you? Is it easy to find people who are willing to listen?
- What sorts of situations come up in children's work when people need listening to?

Exercise

Find another person with whom to practise encouraging listening. Each think about a situation that presents some problem that you are happy to share – perhaps about a child you work with or some other subject concerned with your job or training. Take turns to tell each other about the problem. Each of you has five minutes.

Use 'encouraging' listening. At the end of each turn, share with one another what the experience has been like. What was it like to be the listener and what was it like to be listened to attentively?

Observation

Become aware of the quality of listening in your place of work, college, home or elsewhere.

- During the course of a week, be on the look-out for any time when someone listens carefully and attentively to another person and the effect that this has. (The speaker can be either adult or child; so can the listener.) Does this happen frequently?
- Look out for interruptions when someone is speaking. What happens? How does the speaker react?
- Practise encouraging listening if an opportunity comes up where you feel it would be helpful. Make notes about what happened, why you thought encouraging listening should be used and how the speaker reacted.

BEING AN ENCOURAGING LISTENER: KEY POINTS

- Sometimes in nursery work people – adults and children – just need to be listened to. They do not need questions, advice or opinions. These can come later if necessary.
- Just being listened to can encourage a person to communicate what is on their mind and can sometimes help them to sort out problems for themselves. It can also help them to calm down if they are feeling flustered.
- The main ways to be an encouraging listener are: not to interrupt, to keep the flow of speech going by using encouraging words, sounds and nods, to look at the person while they are talking and not to make your contribution until they have finished.

5 Feedback

The psychologists who developed ways of thinking about interpersonal communication and the *social skills* involved, based some of their ideas on *practical skills,* such as using tools or driving a car. An important concept for understanding practical skills is feedback. Feedback is information that is fed back to you as a direct result of your actions, the signs that tell you how you are doing and lead you to adjust your performance as you go along.

For example, if you are cutting a channel in a piece of wood you may *feel* that the wood is softer than you first thought and also *see* that the chisel is cutting too deeply. Both represent feedback about your action and cause you almost automatically to lighten the pressure of your hand on the chisel. To take another example, in the car you look at the speedometer and notice that it is over 70 mph. This information is feedback about how fast you are driving and, as a result, you take your foot off the accelerator, the car goes slower and the speedometer shows your new speed.

Feedback in communication

The concept of feedback is also used in relation to interpersonal communication. Here feedback is used for all the verbal and non-verbal 'messages' that pass between two people in the course of an interaction. These have an effect on how and what they communicate to each other.

In interpersonal communication feedback can be either *positive* or *negative*. When you listen in an encouraging way (see Chapter 4) you are giving the other person positive feedback in the form of encouraging sounds, nods, smiles and words. They are aware of these 'messages' which assure them that you are interested in what they say and that it is all right to go on talking. If you were to frown or turn away, the other person would feel you were not interested in them or were even hostile towards them – you would be giving them negative feedback which would have its own negative results. They might, for example, stop talking altogether, or they might become aggressive in order to get their message through.

Here are some more examples of feedback:

- A childminder can see that a child does not understand what she is telling him because he looks puzzled. She finds a different way of explaining to him, using simpler words.

- A nursery nurse tells a father about a forthcoming visit from the nursery doctor when his child can be examined. As she speaks she sees, from his expression, that the father is unnecessarily alarmed. So she reassures him that this is just a routine developmental check-up, available for all the nursery children. The father visibly relaxes.
- A mother is worried about her child having too much sleep at the nursery. She decides that the Nursery Officer, who is smiling, is not taking her complaint seriously – and raises her voice. The Nursery Officer stops smiling and apologizes. The mother starts to speak in a more normal tone of voice.
- A junior play worker wants to tell a colleague about an idea she has for publicizing a fund-raising event. She starts, hesitantly at first, but she sees from her colleague's reaction that he is interested in what she has to say. The colleague does not interrupt, looks towards her and smiles in agreement. She is encouraged to develop her idea and tell him all about it.

Such feedback passes backwards and forwards during all interpersonal communication, letting both parties know how their messages are being received. Sometimes people are aware of the feedback they are giving to other people, but sometimes they are less conscious of how they are coming across. For example, with straightforward verbal feedback, such as 'What a good idea' or 'I don't understand', the speaker is conscious of the message they are sending. With non-verbal feedback (see pages 8–15), such as frowns, smiles or fidgeting, they may be less aware of the 'messages' they are sending out.

Communicating by telephone

Perhaps the main reason people find it difficult to leave a message on an answerphone is that they receive no feedback whatsoever. After the tone you are on your own, and it can feel like talking into thin air. We all expect – and need – feedback in everyday communication. But an answerphone cannot support our communication in the way we are used to, simply because it is not a person: talking to an answerphone is not interpersonal communication! Even an ordinary telephone conversation can sometimes present problems because the feedback received is so limited compared with what we are accustomed to in face-to-face conversations.

Imagine a childminder using the phone to ask a mother if she is going to bring her child in today – it is after the time the child usually arrives and the childminder wants to go out shopping. She will wait in if the child is going to come, but otherwise she would like to get out before the shops are crowded. Over the telephone she gets no feedback from the mother's body language or facial expressions. She cannot see her look of dismay, and the despondent shrug of her shoulders so she does not adjust what she says accordingly. If she had been able to observe these signs, she might have asked if there was any problem. As it is she is rather short with the mother and tells her that she cannot wait much longer.

But even on the phone there is some feedback, over and above the verbal communication, the actual words which are used (see Chapter 2). People use their voices in various ways, intentionally or otherwise. They pause, hesitate, speak quickly or slowly, they are quiet or loud, they sigh, click their tongues, laugh, yawn, let their voices rise to a higher pitch or fall lower. All of these non-verbal communications are feedback that can be picked up on the telephone and which can affect the way a sensitive listener responds.

Using the telephone

- Because telephone calls deprive both sides of feedback, it is wiser not to use the telephone to communicate sensitive material – problems about a child, for example – unless it is absolutely necessary.
- You need to listen even more carefully on the telephone than in everyday conversation. Be especially alert to how people are speaking as well as to the words that are used.
- Remember that the other person cannot see you either, and they have no clues from your body language as to what you mean. So you need to express what you have to say very clearly.
- It is useful to be really sure of what you have to say before you make a call. Start by greeting the other person, say who you are and the main thing you are phoning about: for example, 'Hello, this is June Grey from Hillside Play Centre. I'm ringing about paying for the minibus we hired last week.'

Exercises

Sit back to back with a partner, so that you cannot see each other, and carry out some of the following telephone calls. Take turns to play each part.

- A member of staff rings the suppliers to ask why washing-up liquid and other cleaning materials have not been delivered. They were ordered a month ago. Staff are constantly having to go out to buy cleaning things.
    The person at the other end cannot recall receiving the order. She needs to know when it was sent and other details.
- A mother rings a playgroup to tell them that her son does not want to come in because something has upset him at the playgroup. She does not know what it is, but he is really upset. She wants to know if anything untoward has happened that staff are aware of and asks what she should do.
    The play worker is puzzled. She cannot think of anything. She would like to talk to the mother face to face and thinks that she should see the child and talk to him, also.

- Do you think that you are more or less aware of feedback in interactions with babies and children, than of feedback in interactions with adults?
- Are there any differences in the sort of feedback received from babies, children and adults? If so, what are they?
- Why is it important to be alert to feedback in early years and play work?

Observation

- Be on the look-out for feedback given to children about their communications and any feedback they give to other people.
- Spend 15 minutes watching a television play or 'soap', concentrating on one character and the feedback that they give to others about their communications. Do they welcome communication? Block it? Understand it? How do they give feedback, verbally or non-verbally?

Reflecting back

Reflecting back is a special form of feedback which is useful to have at your command when you need to let someone know that you have heard and understood them.

Reflecting back is when you repeat to the speaker the main thing which he or she has just said, as though you are a mirror for them. Although this sounds as though the other person might find what you say boring, or obvious, you will find that in the right circumstances people welcome reflecting back as a demonstration that you have really heard and understood them.

With practice it becomes easy to reflect back without sounding wooden. There is no need to repeat everything that is said, just the main points, in your own words. Here are some examples.

> *Father* (unavoidably late and rather agitated): I've been trying to get you all day to say I'd be late but I couldn't get through, the phone was always engaged.
> *Play worker* (reassuringly): You tried again and again but we were always engaged.

Reflecting back is useful in this case because the worker lets the father know that she appreciates that he has tried to cooperate. This is not the only sort of feedback a worker could give in this situation. How the worker responds depends on her judgement about the best outcome in this incident. For example, if the father was continually late, the worker might have chosen to confront him about this (we shall look at confrontation in Chapter 11). Or, if the father had a lot to say about the reasons for his lateness (say, his wife had been in a car accident) the worker might have chosen to listen to him attentively and encouragingly without reflecting back. Sometimes a speaker just wants to be listened to.

Here are two more examples of reflecting back:

Child (new and rather shy, showing a picture): This is my mum, and this is my dad and this is my baby and this is me in my house.
Childminder: You've done a picture of all the people who live in your house.

Again this is not the only way of responding. The minder could have asked a question, or made a suggestion or said something about her own family. But reflecting back is reassuring for someone who is shy. In this case it tells the child that they have been heard and focuses the conversation on what is interesting him or her at this moment. The minder could move on to other sorts of responses, later.

Mother: He's already had his medicine this morning, but could you give him a spoonful after his other meals?
Nursery nurse: OK – you want me to give him one spoonful after dinner and another after tea?

This worker is using reflecting back to check that she has understood the instructions she has been given. It gives the mother a chance to correct any misunderstandings.

Exercise

Find a partner and take it in turns to talk about:

- last weekend, what you most enjoyed, what you least enjoyed and why; or
- your placement (or work) with children; what you most enjoy, what you least enjoy and why.

Allow each other five minutes to talk. The task of the listener is to reflect back – the speaker should make the task easy by stopping frequently to give the listener a chance to reflect back.

This may feel artificial (it is!) but it gives you an opportunity to experience and practise reflecting back.

Exchange how you found the experience, both as speaker and as listener.

Practice

- In your placement or at work choose an occasion in conversation with a child to use some reflecting back. How does the child respond?
- Use reflecting back in your conversation with an adult when this seems appropriate and notice how this affects your communication.

Points to discuss or think about

'Communication comes naturally to people, there's no need to think about what you do or say.' What do you think about this point of view?

Reflecting back with children

Reflecting back can also be used when you are playing with children and want to give a child encouragement and companionship, following the child's lead rather than introducing ideas and games of your own.

Children's 'special times'

'Special times' is the name given to one way of reflecting back, which takes place when you are playing with children. It was developed by Rachel Pinney as therapy for children with special needs, but the approach can also be used in work with 'normal' children, particularly when they need individual attention.

When 'special times' is used therapeutically, the adult starts by letting the child know that they are to have a special time together when the child can do whatever they wish. The adult also tells the child that they will make sure that the child will come to no danger. The adult then pays complete attention to the child, feeding back to them whatever they are doing: 'Now you're emptying the box ... You want me to hold the teddy,' and so on. Sometimes the feedback is verbal, describing the child's activities in words, but it can also be non-verbal, consisting of smiles, sounds and actions. The play is directed completely by the child and the adult plays whatever part the child wishes, following the child's cues. For example, the child hands the adult a tea cup and the adult has an appreciative drink. The adult does not make any suggestion – or attempt – to take the play further unless the child shows that this is required. In this sort of play it would be quite inappropriate for the worker to say, 'Can I have a biscuit, as well?' It is quite possible that the child might hand the adult several pretend cups of tea, one after the other and be very pleased with the repetitions.

Children use their special times in different ways. The important thing is that they have the total attention and companionship of the adult for this time.

The special times approach may be used if 'normal' children seem to need some extra attention. It is especially useful when you are getting to know a new child, or just for getting to know a child better. More than anything it means being very attentive to the child, taking on their point of view and, for the time being, sharing their interests rather than imposing your own.

Naturally, as the name implies, the special times approach is for 'special times'. It is not always possible to give extended one-to-one time to one particular child. Also it is often inappropriate that your activities together should be directed by the child. There are many occasions when you make the decisions about a child's activities. For example, you decide when it is time for a story or for lunch. In early years work you may join in their activities with a particular purpose of your own; it could be to do some colour matching or to work on shapes. You may want to tell them about something particularly interesting that has happened to you.

Nevertheless, it is useful to be able to communicate with children in this special way, giving them feedback that they are understood and accepted, while at the same time you have the opportunity to understand them better. It is also a corrective to intruding in their play and taking over its direction. If you allow children to take the lead it is as though they are using you as a very sophisticated plaything. You may be surprised at the length of time for which they are able to sustain their play without any suggestions from you.

Practice

- Try to make some opportunities in which you work with a child, reflecting back their play, allowing them to take the lead. What happens? Or
- Allow a young child to take you for a walk round a park. Let them look at things, retrace their steps, linger where they wish, run, or sit down for as long as they like. Just follow where they lead. Only step in if they are going into danger or causing damage.

What do you learn from these exercises about the child and about yourself? How difficult is it to allow the child to take the lead?

You pick up what the baby notices

Points to discuss or think about

Do you think there are any advantages and any disadvantages in working in this way, reflecting back children's play, allowing them to take the lead?

'Labelling' as reflecting back

A form of reflecting back is carried out quite unselfconsciously by mothers with their babies and toddlers (and probably by sensitive nursery workers and by fathers as well).

Research has shown that mothers often comment on their babies' experience, as it happens. For example, the mother notices that the baby's attention is attracted to a bird outside the window and says, 'It's a birdy, isn't it? Yes, a bird having a drink of water.' Or she sees that the baby's attention is attracted to a noise outside and says, 'What's that? ... What can you hear? It's a car, isn't it? ... Daddy's car.'*

The person close to the baby shares their experience and names it or labels it for them: 'You like that, don't you? ... Mm, that's good,' says the nursery nurse, as the baby guzzles happily, or 'You're trying to get hold of my hair, aren't you?' as she avoids the baby's grasp.

Labelling is a sort of reflecting back – taking the baby's experience and playing it back to them. It is different from pointing out and naming something that is interesting you. In fact, it is often difficult to get babies or young toddlers to pay attention to something 'out there' which they have not noticed for themselves; for example, they may not follow the direction of your finger if you point towards something.

Because of labelling, repeated on many occasions, babies learn that there are words used to match their experience; for example, the experience of seeing a dog is often accompanied by their carer naming a dog. This is one of the means by which children acquire language.

When you label what a child is seeing, or experiencing through other senses, then you are seeing things from the child's point of view – an essential skill for people who work with young children and vital for sensitive communication.

Points to discuss or think about

Can you see any similarities between the labelling that adults carry out when they are interacting with babies and the 'special times' approach described earlier?

*See Rudolph Schaffer's *Mothering*, pages 81–2 (Fontana, 1985)

Observation

Watch someone, a parent or a nursery worker, feeding a baby (from about eight months) or a toddler, or playing with them. Be on the look-out for the adult following the child's lead and labelling what the child is seeing, hearing, feeling or tasting.

FEEDBACK: KEY POINTS

- In interpersonal communication, 'feedback' constantly passes between the people who are communicating.
- Feedback tells you if your message is getting through, as you intended. In the light of feedback, people modify their communication.
- Listening in an encouraging way gives positive feedback, which encourages a speaker to continue.
- Another form of feedback is *reflecting back*. To reflect back what someone says you repeat back to them, often in your own words, the content of their message to you. This assures them that they are properly understood. Reflecting back can be especially useful if another person is agitated or shy, or if you need to check that you have understood their message.
- A special way of playing with children is to feed back to them what they are doing and to follow their lead totally. This is especially useful for getting to know a child better.
- Related to feedback is when adults 'label' babies' and children's experience for them, giving a name to what the child is experiencing.

6 Reflecting feelings

In all forms of work with children you are often in close contact with people who are in the grip of strong emotions: a child who is delighted because she can at last ride a bicycle without stabilizers; a mother who telephones you from hospital as she anxiously waits for her baby to recover from an anaesthetic; the child upset because his parents have just left him with you for the first time; the mother who is cross because a new coat has gone missing from the nursery. The messages that pass between people are often about personal feelings and need a sensitive response.

What are feelings?

One way of thinking about feelings is as physical sensations and reactions. So if you hear sad news, you may feel a 'lump in your throat' as the muscles tighten and you find it hard to swallow. Or when you are very anxious, such as before an exam or an interview, you may experience your anxiety as an uneasy crampy feeling in your stomach.

Feelings are different from thoughts, although many people mix them up in everyday conversation.

A teacher might say, 'What do you feel we should do – start on the colour table today or leave it until next week?' He is asking for your thoughts, opinions and ideas, not about your emotions. Or a childminder says, 'I feel that children need a well-balanced meal at midday,' when, in fact, this is what she *believes* or *thinks* rather than what she feels. At the same time feelings may come into the picture. The minder may feel pride at providing properly for the children or anxious that she is not doing well enough.

Although thoughts and feelings are different, there are often connections between them, because each can affect the other. If people who work with children learn that a child is mistreated at home, some may *feel* angry, others depressed. But they do not necessarily act on how they feel; what they *think* about the situation can have a bigger effect on their actions. A play worker who has reason to believe that a child is mistreated, may think to himself, 'If I show my feelings while I am talking to the child's mother it will make things worse. So I'd better calm down and carry on in a way that is best for the child.' When he reacts in this way his thoughts are controlling his responses, rather than his feelings.

The feelings that can be observed in early years and play work are enormously varied. Over a few weeks they might include joy, anger, sadness, affection, friendliness, pride, grief, anger, irritation, trust and worry. In the course of your work it is necessary to be aware of them in other people and in yourself. They can be important messages in their own right; they can also be sources of interference – stopping people from expressing what they want to say or from hearing other people properly (see pages 29–30).

Recognizing feelings

Feelings can be expressed both verbally and non-verbally. Someone can tell you, 'I feel so happy,' when you already know because they are smiling broadly. Here are some of the ways feelings are expressed without words (non-verbally):

- a little girl skips along the pavement;
- a child reaches up and strokes your face;
- a friend gives another a hug;
- a mother sighs as she lifts a basket of shopping;
- a father frowns when you tell him you need a cake for the nursery party;
- a child quickly covers her mouth with her hand when you ask, 'Who spilt the orange juice?'

These are all signs of emotion which help you to understand something about the other person's feelings. But they are signs only, and do not give you a complete understanding of what is happening. Rather than jumping to conclusions, you need to be careful and check out your interpretation in other ways. The frowning father (above) may have just remembered that he has forgotten something for his older child to take for a school sale, or that money is short this week or that his wife is in hospital ... he may have a thousand and one reasons for frowning. His frowning does not necessarily mean that he feels hostile or uncooperative towards you.

Points to discuss or think about

- List as many emotions as you can (some of them may seem very similar to others). Are there any which you are not likely to meet in the course of your work?
- Which non-verbal behaviour would suggest to you that someone is experiencing the following feelings: depression, worry, affection, glee, fear? Remember that emotions can be shown on the face, in movement and posture, vocally and by eye contact (see pages 8–15).

Responding to feelings

When people who work with children notice someone else's feelings, happy or otherwise, they can respond in different ways. Here are three of them:

- *They may ignore the feelings altogether.* For example, a mother brings her child into the classroom, her head is hanging (perhaps she is crying), and she takes the child's coat off and hands the nursery nurse his apple without a word. She usually chats. The worker feels embarrassed, she does not know what to say, so she keeps quiet and bends down to do up the child's shoelace so that she does not have to look at the mother. The mother is desperate to talk about a problem at home, but does not know how to start. She cannot make eye contact with the worker, who is busy with the shoelace and, after hesitating for a moment, she goes away feeling even worse.
- *They may deny the feelings.* For example, it is Saturday morning in the adventure playground, an hour or so before the children arrive. Yasmin did not really want to come into work today. A colleague comes in with a bounce in her step and gives her a cheery 'Hello' and begins to sing as she puts the kettle on. Yasmin says, 'Oh no, you can't be as cheerful as all that.'

  As well as denying cheerful feelings, it is also possible – and perhaps more usual – to deny sad feelings as the next example shows: Yasmin is on the way home, feeling really gloomy and her friend calls over from the other side of the street, 'Cheer up, it may never happen!'
- *But they can also acknowledge the feelings and reflect them back.* A childminder is busy with a baby, changing his nappy. Her own 12 year old comes in from school scowling, slams the door and throws her books down on the table. The minder says, 'You look as though you've had a really bad day ... I'll be with you in a minute.'

By saying this she communicates that she has picked up something of what her daughter is feeling and that she accepts this. Acknowledging and reflecting back emotions shows respect for what another person is experiencing. In other words, it shows respect for that person. If a child comes crying to you with a cut knee, 'You've cut your knee and it hurts badly,' is one appropriate response as you start to take action. It reflects back what has happened and what the child is feeling about it – you are letting him know that you understand and accept him. Being accepted is an important experience for children, which helps them to feel secure and confident about themselves.

Some people might object that it would be better to try to cheer up a hurt child or to tell him that his knee 'doesn't hurt that much'. This would be to deny the child's own feelings. I have noticed that when adults deny that children are upset, they often cry all the louder – as though to convince their listeners of how bad they feel, to get through to them that this is really

It is important to acknowledge children's feelings and not deny them

important and needs attention. It is also true that if children are constantly made to feel ashamed of crying, they come to believe that sharing painful feelings is not permitted and may well carry this understanding into adult life. If you acknowledge and reflect their feelings, they are comforted and know that you share their understanding of the situation (and they often stop crying).

Partings

Sad or angry feelings are frequently displayed when parents first leave young children in the care of somebody else. In early years work these partings must be handled with sensitivity. If at all possible there should be a period of time for settling in. Children need to get used to new adults, to being one of a group of children, to having a routine which is different from home and to being in an unfamiliar setting with strange furniture and unfamiliar toys.

A gradual approach is probably the best for settling in. To start with there should be short visits with one or other parent. Because the parent is present, children feel secure getting to know you and their new surroundings.

During these first visits you can start by just watching the parent taking care of the child – taking their coat off, taking them to the toilet, helping them to wash their hands. Then gradually you can take over some of these tasks while the parent is present and watching you. In this way, children see that their parents trust you.

You can use this time to find out more about the children. It is important to ask a parent about the child's likes and dislikes with regard to food and other parts of their daily routine. Are there people at home, or pets, whom the child might refer to? What does the child call them? You need this information to understand what the child is talking about. Are there special words or signs they use for going to the toilet? Have they got a comfort object, such as a teddy or piece of blanket, which they turn to in distress – and what do they call it? You can make a written record of this information, so that it is there for any other staff who come in contact with the child and as a reminder for yourself.

All of this knowledge will help you to communicate better. When the first parting occurs, you will be in a better position to receive the child's messages and to understand their point of view. And because they have had time to get used to you, the child will be in a better position to understand you.

On the first occasion that a parent goes away, they should leave the child for a few minutes only, letting them know that they will return soon. They can, over a few days, increase the time they are away.

Even when all these gradual steps are taken, some children are still upset when their parents leave. And in other cases an emergency of some sort may mean that children are left with strange carers, without any preparation at all. When children are upset at parting you should acknowledge how they feel, as well as reassuring them that their parents will be back later. They may be especially clinging to you, during the first days of separation and, as far as possible, you should allow this and make use of the opportunity to get to know them better. They will gain security as they come to realize that you understand them, accept them – feelings and all – and respond to them when they need you. Once they feel secure they will be ready to venture away from you and find interesting games and playmates, knowing that you are at hand.

Reflecting adults' feelings

Sensitive communication also involves awareness of adults' feelings and the ability and willingness to reflect them. You may need to show someone – an angry colleague or an upset father – that you know how they feel by reflecting their feelings back to them. So if someone says, 'I'm going to see my mother tonight ...' and sighs deeply, replying, 'You're not feeling too good about it,' communicates that you have picked up an important message. You are reflecting *feelings* back to the speaker. This is different from reflecting back *content*.

To take the above example again, if someone says, sighing deeply, 'I'm going to see my mother tonight ...', and you respond cheerfully, 'So you're off to Fulham,' ignoring the sigh, then you are ignoring the *feelings* behind what is said and reflecting only the *content* of the words. This may not be an adequate response for the other person. It is necessary to accept that the other person feels as they do – even if you think that their feelings are unrealistic. For example, if a mother seems over-anxious about the possibility that her child has got chickenpox it does not help her to say, 'You're worried in case he's got chickenpox!', in a tone of complete scorn, suggesting that she is stupid to let such a trivial matter upset her. If the mother is extremely anxious you should first show that you understand and accept how she is feeling. You may then want to provide some realistic information, for example, that chickenpox is unpleasant, but not dangerous, for a five year old.

In providing feedback, go carefully, in case you have misunderstood or have over-estimated how the other person is feeling. For example, say, 'You look a bit down,' rather than, 'You look absolutely devastated,' or 'You're worried in case he's got chickenpox,' rather than, 'You're feeling terribly anxious about it.'

In some circumstances, you may feel that acknowledging someone's feelings would leave you out of your depth. You may believe that it would be difficult to handle the situation if the other person were to say more about what was troubling them: for example, if you thought that a mother was trying to confide in you that her child was being abused. In cases like this, and if you think that the situation is serious for the child who is involved, it is better to let a senior colleague know what is happening and let them deal with the situation than try to handle it yourself.

In summary, if you want to encourage the process of communication, which includes the communication of feelings, try to see things from the other person's point of view, accept their messages and let them know that you accept them. This may not come easily to start with but practice helps.

Points to discuss or think about

- Have you ever had the experience of someone ignoring your feelings? Has anyone ever denied your feelings? Have you ever noticed either of these happening to somebody else? What was the reaction?
- Are there any problems about acknowledging other people's feelings in your work? Are there any disadvantages if you do not acknowledge others' feelings?

Exercise

Practise reflecting back feelings with another person. Think of some problem you have in your work or training, which you are willing to share with someone else.

Find a partner and each take turns, for about five minutes, to share your problems. When you are the speaker remember to stop to give the other person a chance to reflect back. The listener should reflect back feelings and use encouraging listening. Then change roles so that each person has a turn to be listener and speaker.

After you have each had a turn, share with each other how you found the experiences of being a listener and of being listened to. Were there any learning points?

Practice

If suitable opportunities arise, practise reflecting back feelings in your communications with adults and with children.

Notice what happens: how are the feelings communicated to you? How does
the other person respond when you reflect back? Are you satisfied with how you
handle things?

Observation

Watch a television play or 'soap' and follow one of the main characters. What
feelings does the character communicate? How do other people react to the
feelings? Are the feelings accepted, reflected back, denied or ignored?

Sad events in children's lives

Sooner or later staff come across children who are upset because of something that has happened in their family, perhaps the loss of a parent through
illness, death or marriage breakdown. Workers find this painful. They are
aware that they cannot change things for the child and there is the possibility
that they are reminded of sad events from their own past.

Because of their own painful feelings, some staff may try to avoid any
communication with the child about what has happened. This is unwise: if
children are already feeling sad – or anxious or angry – to deny their feelings
by ignoring them or 'brushing them under the carpet' may confuse children,
thus adding to their unhappiness. Accepting feelings, and letting the child
know that you do so, is more helpful. This is not suggesting that you raise
painful subjects with children but that if they do so themselves, then you
should accept their communications.

Sometimes children ask questions about subjects like death and illness,
which you do not know how to deal with. They may make you feel anxious
because you are not sure if the children are old enough to understand or to
cope with the answer. It is always best to answer these sorts of questions in a
straightforward way. If you do not do so, you run the risk of confusing the
children. You can also make them more fearful if they suspect that the
answer to their question must be devastating, on the grounds that you keep
it from them. In cases such as these, answer quite simply and truthfully and
be ready to answer any further questions that arise (see also pages 68–70).

You may find that in the course of your work you become quite involved
in the events of a child's life and in their feelings, and that this involvement
is difficult to bear. If this happens, talking things over with an attentive colleague or a more senior member of staff can help you to sort out and accept
your own feelings about the situation. It is then easier to give the child the
acceptance and support which they need.

Points to discuss or think about

- A girl who attended a playscheme for children with disabilities died. A few months after her death there was a special ceremony of remembrance for her. Children and staff planted a tree together, spoke about the dead child and thought about her. The children had made decorations which they hung on the tree during the ceremony.

   What do you think about this approach? How would you have felt as a member of staff? Should children with disabilities be treated differently when it comes to talking to them about death and other sad events? Do you think that it would be appropriate to have a memorial ceremony in a nursery? For a teacher? For a child? What lies behind your answers to these questions?

- You are a childminder. A child you've looked after for two years dies. The other children ask about her. Do you reply:

   'No more questions, just get on with your dinner'; or
   'Tracy's mum has moved and Tracy won't be coming back any more'; or
   'Tracy was ill and died.'

   Take each answer in turn: what problems do you see arising from each answer? What are the advantages? Is there a better answer? What would you say?

- You are a play worker. Gary comes up to you, beaming, and says, 'My dad's coming out of prison tomorrow?' (You did not know he was in prison.) Do you reply:

   'Oh, isn't that lovely'; or
   'Don't tell stories'; or
   'Would you like to play football tonight?'

   Or do you make some other reply? Why do you make this choice?

Observation

Spend some time observing children and pay especial attention to their feelings. What feelings do you think you observe? How do you recognize them? Do you think that the feelings are accepted, denied or ignored by adults and by other children?

REFLECTING FEELINGS: KEY POINTS

- Feelings play a large part in interpersonal communication, so be alert for the messages – verbal or non-verbal – that adults and children provide about their feelings. Be observant.
- Feed back that you have picked up the feelings; that is, identify the feelings and reflect them back to the other person. This shows that you accept the other person.
- Do not ignore or deny other people's feelings.
- If a situation seems serious and you do not feel confident about handling it yourself, let a senior colleague know.
- Answer children's questions about sad or painful subjects as simply and directly as you can.

7 Communications about yourself

So far we have concentrated on feedback and especially on all those encouraging, positive responses you can give to help people to communicate well when they are talking about themselves and their concerns. But there are also occasions at work when you want to add your own input to a conversation, to talk about yourself and your interests. When you tell another person something about yourself which they did not know before, you are making a disclosure about yourself. It is something you do frequently with your family and friends. You tell them what sort of a day you have had, how you are feeling, what you are looking forward to. You may talk about important things that have happened in the past or about problems you are having at present. It is good to be open, to share experience and this goes for work as well as home.

Of course, you do not want to share everything with everyone. You can probably remember keeping information to yourself – not because you were being secretive but because you decided that this was not the appropriate person, or perhaps the appropriate time, for sharing. Often you make these choices almost instinctively, without having to think very much about them. However, there are times when you need to make decisions about any self-disclosure you might make at work. This is because, as well as being a normal part of communication, some types of self-disclosure may stand in the way of what you are trying to achieve in your work. You may, therefore, have to consider when and to whom you make disclosures about yourself, and what it is appropriate to disclose.

When disclosure is helpful

Here are some points to help you decide if self-disclosure is helpful.

Is the information appropriate?

Some personal information is more weighty, more serious, than other personal information; disclosing serious information about yourself may be inappropriate, as the following contrasting examples show.

- A play worker is talking to one of the children. She says, 'You went to the seaside on Saturday? I went to the seaside too – we went to Marshbanks. There's too much mud there for my liking.'
- A nursery nurse says to a mother, 'I forgot to take my anti-depressant this morning and everything is getting me down!'

In the first example the play worker makes a disclosure about herself. She tells the child what she did on Saturday and the child would not otherwise have known this. This disclosure could be the beginning of an interesting conversation. I leave you to imagine some of the possible consequences of the second, highly unlikely, example! However, it points to an important lesson: the more serious or weighty the disclosure, the more difficulty there may be about its appropriateness. Serious personal information is not for sharing without good reason. (Notice this is not to say that serious material must never be shared, but that there must be an equally serious reason for doing so.)

Disclosure can make for closeness

Telling someone something about yourself makes you less distant and may help them to feel ready to share their experience with you. You may feel you need to encourage a shy person, so that you can get to know one another better, and talking a little about your own experience is one way to do it. (We shall see in the next chapter that asking a series of questions, which is sometimes used to encourage conversation, may in fact make conversation more difficult.)

For example, you are a playgroup worker, sitting next to a volunteer on a coach trip to the seaside. The volunteer is new to the group and seems to be rather shy. One way in which you can help her to feel more at ease is to give her the opportunity to talk about herself. Saying something about yourself like, 'This reminds me of school trips when I was little ...' could start the ball rolling. This is not the same as 'hogging the conversation', so long as you leave space for her to join in.

There is also a place for sharing your own experience in your conversations with children. You can foster communication with a child by saying something about yourself – your experience, feelings and thoughts – which can be more effective than a stream of questions in helping the conversation along (see page 65). It can also introduce interesting subjects which stretch children's understanding and widen their horizons.

Points to discuss or think about

- Can you remember interesting adults from your own childhood? What sorts of things did they tell you about?
- Did they have any belongings, any special objects, that seemed to arouse your curiosity and lead into an interesting conversation – photographs, perhaps, or knick-knacks, jewellery or other treasures? Bearing in mind the age of the children you work with, is there any way that you could use some of your own personal belongings – things you take out of your pocket or handbag – to start conversations with children? Is there anything you could bring from home which might interest them?
- In your experience, is it easier to make conversation (not just a set of questions and answers) with children or with adults?

Sharing experience can show understanding

By talking about your own experience it is possible to show that you understand the other person's problem. An early years worker says to a mother, 'He's still waking you up during the night? I know what it's like – I had the same with mine. I used to long for six hours' undisturbed sleep.' The mother knows that the worker appreciates her situation.

Remember, though, that the experiences of two people which on the surface sound alike may, in fact, be very different. You may not really understand the feelings of another person in a difficult situation, even though you have lived through something that seems similar yourself. For example, the feelings involved in one divorce may be totally unlike those involved in another. Do not, therefore, claim that you fully understand what is happening to somebody else, on the grounds that you have been through it yourself. Be ready to listen.

When disclosure is unhelpful

Disclosure can be a burden

Sharing your problems may mean burdening other people with them. This may be acceptable between friends, but it is not appropriate where your relationship is a professional one. At work, your job is to be of service to the children and their families; they have no similar obligations towards you.

Similarly, self-disclosure can shift the focus of a conversation to your interests, at a point when this may not be useful. If a mother wants to talk to you about her baby and the problems she has with feeding, telling her how your niece, of the same age, is now on solids could be a distraction, suggesting that you are not interested in the difficulties that the mother is experiencing.

There are many times in your work, as we saw earlier, when encouraging listening and reflecting back are the most useful responses and should be used rather than disclosing information about yourself.

Taking too large a part in the conversation

Sometimes people take too large a part in the conversation, talking a great deal about themselves without allowing other people a chance to contribute. This is boring for others and may lead them to feel under-valued by the person concerned. Sometimes early years workers may feel that they have to keep up a stream of talk with children, because they have heard that this is the way to encourage them to develop language. Taking turns is also important and space needs to be made for the children's share in conversation, using the ways covered in the earlier chapters.

Friends or friendly?

Some personal statements may suggest that you see yourself as a 'friend', rather than 'friendly'. It is important to be clear about your relationship with people you meet at work. There is a difference between your relationship with personal friends and that which you have with parents or colleagues: you choose your friends, but not your professional relationships. Friends have a fairly equal relationship based on liking to be with one another. But relationships with colleagues, parents and children are not personal choices. Sometimes you may even find yourself working with people you do not really like. Personal friendships can develop at work but working relationships are based primarily on providing a service for children and parents and on cooperating with colleagues. Behaving differently with different parents and children, by disclosing more about yourself to some than to others, suggests that you prefer some over others, that you have favourites. This can lead to other parents or children feeling excluded and to the suggestion that there are 'cliques'. This is not to say that 'friendliness' – sensitivity, encouragement, warmth – is out of place – in fact, it is essential – but that friendliness should, to the best of your ability, be shown equally to all the people you work with.

Points to discuss or think about

- Bearing in mind what you have just read, how appropriate would it be for someone in early years or play work to say to a parent:
  'Monday again, I didn't feel like coming into work this morning.'
  'I'm going to be away for a couple of weeks because I'm getting married.'
  'I spent most of the weekend working for the local Labour/ Conservative/ Liberal Democratic Party.'
  'I know what you mean, I'm widowed myself.'
  'I'm at my wit's end about my father. I feel I ought to stay at home to look afer him, but I need to work for the money.'
  'I'm feeling great today!'
  Which was the most difficult statement to decide about? Why?
- 'You can't make rules about self-disclosure – it depends on the work you're doing and where you're working: if you're a nanny, a childminder, a nursery officer in a hospital, a play worker in an after-school scheme or whatever.' What do you think about this statement?
- 'You can be friends with the parents and you can be friends with your colleagues.' What do you think about this point of view?
- What reasons can you think of for and against nursery workers wearing political badges or religious symbols?
- Should you ever talk to parents or children about any difficulties you are having with colleagues?

Observation

Become aware of the part of self-disclosure in people's conversation. Listen at work and elsewhere, wherever you are. Or watch a play or 'soap' on television and for 15 minutes concentrate on one character. Does the character use encouraging listening, reflecting back, questions or disclosure? Does the character use one more than the other?

Was there anything you specially noticed about the part that self-disclosure plays in communication? How common is it? Do you notice conversations where there is little self-disclosure from either party? What are they like?

COMMUNICATIONS ABOUT YOURSELF: KEY POINTS

- Self-disclosure is giving other people information about yourself which they would not otherwise know.
- Self-disclosure on your part can encourage others to make disclosures about themselves. It can start them talking.
- Self-disclosure can make you seem more approachable.
- Disclosing something about your own experience may suggest that you understand and sympathize with another person's situation. But be careful, as this may be misleading.
- Self-disclosure also has disadvantages. It can burden other people with your problems; change the focus from the other person to yourself; suggest that you are a 'friend' rather than 'friendly'; suggest 'favouritism' if you disclose more to some people than to others.

8   Questions

Skilled interpersonal communication involves many activities: observing and listening, avoiding interference, reflecting back and talking about yourself, your feelings, ideas and experience. This chapter introduces the use of questions and how they can be used in early years and play work. In nursery work, asking questions is a very familiar activity but we are not always aware of the effect that questions, and different sorts of questions, can have on our communications with adults and children – sometimes they help the process along but at other times they can get in the way.

Open and closed questions

Asking questions well is an art in itself – think of a good radio interview compared with one that goes badly. An experienced interviewer just seems to start a conversation going with a simple question then guides it along with further questions, drawing out the experience of the interviewed person. Other interviewers can shut the interviewee up with a stream of questions which get answered briefly or in monosyllables. There is more than one type of question that can be used and the right type can be vital for obtaining full information from the interviewee. A useful way of grouping questions is according to whether they are closed or open.

Closed questions

These are questions that can be answered fairly simply, often with an answer that is short and limited. For example:

    'Did you enjoy the film?'
    'You've drawn a house, haven't you?'
    'Is that a pussy cat?'
    'Do you like mushrooms?'
    'Have you heard their new single?'
    'Would you like the red cup or the blue one?'

The above questions are all closed questions and answers to them may very well consist of only one word: 'Yes', 'No', 'Red' or 'Blue'. If in your work you ask mainly closed questions, someone who is feeling shy, for example, a child, a new parent or new member of staff, may answer with only one word and then it is up to you, once again, to continue the conversation. Another way of saying this is that when you ask closed questions you are taking control of the conversation. Unless the other person is quite assertive, it is not easy for them to make their contribution or to introduce subjects they are interested in.

Open questions

Open questions, on the other hand, give the person you are talking to much more choice in how they answer. They often begin with 'How' or 'Why':

'Why did you want to see me?'
'How did you get the icing smooth like that?'
'How does the new flat compare with where you were before?'
'How do you feel about that?'

The person answering is never limited to 'Yes' or 'No' with open questions; they are given the opportunity to provide longer answers, bringing in additional information and opinions if they wish to do so. This does not mean that you should never use closed questions. They are useful for clarification: for example, 'Did you mean that the window was open all night?' checks that the questioner has understood the situation properly. They are also used for obtaining simple information as in, 'How old is he?' But open questions are better than closed questions if you want to encourage someone to talk about their experience.

Questions that begin with 'How' are less threatening than those that begin with 'Why'. You may notice a small difference in feeling between, 'Why did you send her to nursery?' and 'How did you come to send her to nursery?' The first question asks for reasons and a timid person might feel that there is the risk of giving a wrong answer. 'How did you come to send her to nursery?', on the other hand, is asking about someone's experience, the events that led to a decision, and may seem less threatening.

Exercise

Twenty questions. Find a partner and each write down the name of a child you know. Each person has 20 questions to find out as much as possible about their partner's child – their background, age, gender, likes and dislikes, what sort of child they are, and so on. The only answers allowed are 'Yes' or 'No', so questions must be framed accordingly, that is, they must be closed questions.

When you have each had a turn, try the exercise again, with a different partner; this time you are both allowed to use open questions.

What differences did you notice between the two exercises – as a questioner and as someone providing answers? How did you feel? Did open questions or closed questions give you a better picture of the child?

Helpful questions

Questions can make space for others to talk

Mothers and other caregivers constantly use questions as a way of showing that babies can take their turn in a 'conversation'. 'You like that, don't you?' the mother says to her two-month-old baby, long before there is any chance of the baby responding. Short questions of this sort, tagged on to the end of statements, are often used to indicate to others that it is their turn to join in a conversation. They are called 'tag' questions. 'It was a good film, wasn't it?' you ask or, after giving your opinion, you hand the topic over with a question like, 'You know what I mean?'

Sometimes questions are used to reflect back. Someone says, 'I really like working in the Special Baby Unit,' and her friend answers with a question which reflects back what has just been said, 'You're enjoying it then?', at which the first speaker is invited to continue talking about her experience. Or a worker can use a short question just to keep a child talking: 'I went out with my mum,' says the child. 'Did you?' asks the worker, showing interest. 'Yes, and we saw dad's nan,' continues the child, encouraged by the question.

Questions can make things clear

Sometimes you need to ask questions to clarify a situation – something is not clear, you do not understand or you need extra information. Occasionally, people are diffident about this and are afraid to ask about something in case they look foolish. This is a mistake which can lead to difficulties and confusion.

For example, a new member of staff on a maternity ward is told that a baby is going to have a Guthrie test. She does not know what this is but feels too shy to ask. Later, when she is helping the mother feed the baby, the mother seems to be upset, she asks about the test and if it means that something is wrong with the baby. The nursery nurse's hesitation does not help the situation. Because she does not know about it, she cannot reply that the test is routine and something that all new babies have. Her embarrassment comes across as though there is something she does not wish to talk about, and this is alarming for the mother.

Questions show you are interested

Questions, especially open questions, can show that you have a friendly interest in someone. If there are not too many, they help the other person to relax and talk more easily about themselves. 'Where did you go for your holiday? What was it like?' may start the ball rolling.

When questions are unhelpful

Too many questions

Although questions can show that you are interested in another person, asking too many questions can be daunting, almost inquisitorial. So you need to be ready to use other communication skills if you find yourself in a conversation which seems to be getting stuck. You can say something about your own experience, such as, 'I can never manage the icing properly so I get my friend to do it for me,' followed by another question if necessary: 'How did you learn to do it?' Or you can use reflecting back: 'You really enjoy doing it,' and wait for an answer.

Too many questions can put an end to communication

Sensitive questions

We have all, at some time or other, met people who ask questions about things which are none of their business, questions which touch on sensitive areas and which give rise to resentment. In most early years or play work, questions about another person's private life are not necessary and should not arise. But sometimes senior workers need to ask sensitive questions in order to clarify a situation.

For example, it may seem from something a father has just said that a child's mother has left home. A worker may decide to clarify this with a question: 'I don't know if I got it right, but is Emma's mother not living with you and Emma now?' If the father wished to convey this information, then it is important for the worker to know about it, and the question was justifiable.

Nevertheless sensitive questions can be threatening and intrusive. Before asking a question which is at all sensitive ask yourself:

'Is it essential for me to find out about this? Do I really need to know for the good of the child and in order to carry out my professional duties?'

'Am I the right person to be asking this question? Perhaps it would be better to talk to a senior worker about any anxiety I have about the child's welfare.'

Asking questions carries responsibilities. Encouraging self-disclosure (see Chapter 7) on sensitive subjects, including by asking questions, carries the responsibility for using the information for the good of the child. If, to take an extreme example, as a result of your questions, someone confides that another adult in the family is abusing a child, then it is your responsibility to pass the information on. This may be to a senior play worker, officer-in-charge, ward sister or headteacher. If you yourself are in charge of an establishment, or are working as a childminder, you should talk to your line manager or to a local authority adviser. You must also tell the mother that you are going to pass the information on (see pages 118–19).

Points to discuss or think about

Two play workers are talking over a coffee. One says to the other, 'I'd never ask parents questions about their private lives, no matter what I thought was happening.' The other replies, 'Well I think I would if I had to. But with children it's different. You should never ask children questions about their families.'
    What would you say if you joined in the conversation? What reasons would you give?

Observation

- Become aware of the part questions play in interpersonal communication in everyday life. Do questions seem to help a conversation along or put a stop to it?
- Watch some interviews on television, or listen to interviews on the radio. Does the interviewer use open or closed questions? Are there any questions which seem to threaten the interviewee? Do you notice any differences between interviewers?

Asking children questions

Asking questions has been used in education for thousands of years. As we have seen, some questions are encouraging and they can help children to communicate. Careful questions can lead pupils to make discoveries for themselves and draw their attention to different aspects of a problem.

Another reason for asking questions is to find out what a child knows or how much they understand: for example, questions about colour, number or size. But asking children certain sorts of questions can become a habit without any real purpose. For example, in nursery work a member of staff might say, 'What a nice house. What colour is it?' Stock questions such as this may be no more than paying the child a little verbal attention in passing, especially if the member of staff does not really need to test if the child can recognize colours.

Researchers have found that when nursery staff use many questions in their conversations with children, the children seem to 'clam up' or they answer only in monosyllables.* Closed questions especially can have this effect. Also researchers have noticed that sometimes the worker concerned hardly seems to listen to the child's answer, but just goes straight on to another question.

On the other hand, reflecting back or labelling (see pages 43–5 and 47) gives children information, shows that you are taking in what they are doing or noticing and encourages them to speak. So saying something like, 'You've painted it all green, except for this bit here, haven't you?' keeps the conversation focused on the child's own activities and leaves space for their contribution to the conversation. And, as always, you can disclose something about yourself to help the conversation along if you wish.

*See *Working with Under-Fives*, David Wood *et al.* (Grant McIntyre, 1980) and *Young Children Learning*, Barbara Tizard and Martin Hughes (Fontana, 1984)

Points to discuss or think about

- Can you remember teachers asking questions when you were at school?
- How did you feel when you were asked questions?
- In your experience, what are the disadvantages connected with asking children questions?

Children's questions

Children can be persistent questioners when they need information for their own purposes and especially when they are puzzled – when something does not make sense according to their present understanding of the world. Children can be interested in many different fields of knowledge, such as the economic system, zoology or the child's own personal history – anything that comes to their notice and arouses their curiosity.

These persistent questions can often be difficult for staff because they do not know the answer to questions like, 'Why doesn't the fly fall off the ceiling?' Or staff can be puzzled by a child's question because they cannot see the world from the child's point of view – they do not fully understand the background of knowledge the child has obtained and they do not know where the gaps in that knowledge are. Often they may not know enough about the children's lives at home to make sense of what they say. In these circumstances, it is worthwhile to be patient and to ask enough questions to discover what it is, exactly, that is puzzling them. Trying to understand a child's point of view and providing the required information is a valuable piece of interpersonal communication. In this way children can find out about the world, expand their knowledge and put right their own misunderstandings.

Exercise

Read the following conversation (which was recorded in real life) and pay special attention to the child's questions. The conversation takes place at home between a mother and a three-year-old girl. A neighbour, Pamela, has just left.

Girl: What did Pamela say?
Mother: She's having to pay everybody else's bills for the window-cleaner 'cause they're all out.
Girl: Why are they all out?
Mother: 'Cause they're working or something.
Girl: Aren't they silly?
Mother: Well you have to work to earn money, don't you?
Girl: Yeah, if they know what day the window-cleaner comes, they should stay in.
Mother: They should stay at home? Well I don't know, they can't always ...
(At this point there is a change in the conversation, but the girl raises the subject again, later.)

Girl: Mummy?

Mother: Mmm.

Girl: Umm ... she can't pay everybody's, er ... all the bills to the window-cleaner can she?

Mother: No she can't pay everybody's bills ... she sometimes pays mine if I'm out.

Girl: 'Cause it's fair.

Mother: Mm, it is.

Girl: Umm, where does she leave the money?

Mother: She doesn't leave it anywhere, she hands it to the window-cleaner when he's finished.

Girl: And then she gives it to us?

Mother: No, no, she doesn't have to pay us.

Girl: Then the window-cleaner gives it to us?

Mother: No, we give the window-cleaner money, he does work for us, and we have to give him money.

Girl: Why?

Mother: Well, because he's been working for us cleaning our windows. He does-n't do it for nothing.

Girl: Why do you have money if you have ... if people clean your windows?

Mother: Well, the window-cleaner needs money, doesn't he?

Girl: Why?

Mother: To buy clothes for his children and food for them to eat.

Girl: Well, sometimes window-cleaners don't have children.

Mother: Quite often they do.

Girl: And something of his own to eat, and for curtains?

Mother: And for paying his gas bills and electricity bill and for paying for petrol for his car. All sorts of things you have to pay for, you see. You have to earn money somehow, and he earns it by cleaning other people's windows and big shop windows and things.

Girl: And the person who got the money gives it to people ...

- What misunderstandings or puzzles does the girl have?
- What information does she acquire?
- What part does the mother play in helping her to learn?
- How useful do you think conversations like these are in developing children's understanding?

This sequence is between a mother and child at home. However, early years staff and play workers can also provide children with useful information, by answering their questions. This is what happened when some playscheme children went for a walk by the river.

In answer to the children's questions, the play worker told them about the different types of water fowl and about their colouring. One child was confused because both ducks and drakes were called ducks. The play worker explained this. She also told the children that a female swan was called a pen. They talked about how the swans would make their way up river, all the way to the next town. The children asked would they fly or would they swim? The play worker answered their questions.

They went further along the bank and stopped for ten minutes to watch the weir. Again there was much conversation and questions from the children. One child asked about a tributary river that could be seen coming in on the further bank. The play worker told him its name and explained how smaller rivers and streams feed into larger rivers which then feed into the sea.*

Observation

Over the next few weeks, be on the look-out for children's questions: single questions or sequences of questions, when a child is determined to find out more or to get at the root of something. If you are involved, answer patiently without changing the subject.

• Describe any sequence of questions that you find interesting.
• Say what lies behind the children's questions – what lack of understanding or need for information.
• Include any difficulties you have in understanding what lies behind the questions – your own puzzlement.

Exercise

Read the following conversation and look carefully at the nursery worker's questions. Do they help the child to communicate? Can you suggest other things that the worker could have said?
  A four-year-old boy is looking at a picture of a rabbit looking at a newspaper. He tells his friend that it is a mouse.

Nursery worker: It isn't a mouse actually. Do you know what it is?
Boy: (*no answer*)
Nursery worker: Do you know how they make a warren?
Boy: What's their name?
Nursery worker: They don't have names, they're just rabbits. Does your daddy read newspapers?
Boy: I've got lots of books.
Nursery worker: Does he read them to you?
Boy: Depends.
Nursery worker: What books does he read to you?
Boy: My brother's name is Ian.
Nursery worker: Put the book away when you've finished.

Observation

Observe an adult with a child or a group of children – it could be an early years worker, a play worker or a parent and child. A meal time could be a good time to choose. Notice what part, if any, questions play. What sort of questions are asked: open questions, closed questions, 'tag' questions (see pages 62–4). How does the child (or children) respond to questions? Do they seem to help the child take part in the conversation?

*From *Care and Play, Out of School*, Pat Petrie (HMSO, 1994)

QUESTIONS: KEY POINTS

- In conversations with adults and children, questions can help communication along or they can get in the way.
- Closed questions usually need one-word answers, for example 'Yes' or 'No', and leave little space for the other person to make a contribution.
- Open questions often begin with 'Why' or 'How' and give the other person much more scope for answering at greater length.
- Some questions, known as 'tag' questions, are not real questions; they are just a way of indicating that you have finished your turn in the conversation. They include phrases like 'Isn't it?' Tag questions are used between adults and in conversations with children, including babies.
- Questions can be used for clarification when you are not sure about something.
- Questions can show that you have a friendly interest in someone.
- Too many questions and insensitive questions are intrusive.
- With children, only ask questions if you really need to know the answer, for example, to carry on your conversation, or if you need to find out what a child knows.
- Otherwise be sparing in asking children questions, and if you ask them listen to the answers.
- Children can ask questions persistently when they are in search of knowledge; be patient, try to understand and give them information.

9 Messages about power and equality

Throughout society there are groups and individuals who by their actions and their interpersonal communications exert power over others. The messages they give about their own superiority and other people's low status can be quite open or largely hidden. Sometimes the people involved are aware of what they are doing but at other times they have not got the slightest idea of the sort of messages their communications convey.

The subject of this chapter is how interpersonal communication can be used to control others and deny them equality. It is also about how to be aware of this and to prevent it happening in early years and play work. We start with open control. Next we examine more indirect, hidden types of control – the messages which result in and sustain social inequality between groups of people: men and women, different ethnic groups, disabled people, young and old, rich and poor and others.

Open control

There are times in nursery work when you have to let people – children, fellow staff, parents – know what is 'acceptable' behaviour or what the rules are. Chapter 11 will suggest how to do this constructively, not by seeking to *control* others, but by treating them with respect, trying to see their point of view and seeking reasonable solutions to problems together.

Sometimes people try to control others quite openly, by threats, by force, by blaming or by moralizing. In such controlling communications the spoken message is, 'Do what I say', together with other messages, spoken and unspoken, that one person is more important than another – whether wiser, stronger or simply more powerful than the other. It is these *controlling* messages which we consider first. These are oppressive communications which express an individual's power, or wish for power, over others, and which are destructive of other people's self-esteem. When a member of staff is disparaging to a child, the child feels insignificant and silly. Being judgemental about someone or moralizing about them shows no respect and eats away at their self-esteem. People can sense when someone is arrogant towards them – the communication gets through. Also the feelings aroused can cause *interference* (see pages 29–30), that is, the listener blocks out part of the intended message and only hears the part that is hurtful.

The following statements all seek to control people and put them down:

- 'I would never have done it like that. Why didn't you ask me first?' (Here the speaker claims superiority and the other person feels stupid or angry, or both.)
- 'It's so lazy, leaving everything lying about. Always clear up before the children go out.' (The implication of this is that the speaker is hard working, well organized and morally superior to the other person.)
- 'How can she eat her dinner, when you've filled her up with biscuits?' (Meaning: 'You don't know as much about looking after children as I do – or perhaps you just don't care.')
- 'Your problem is that you don't listen.' (With the implication that the other person is insensitive, incompetent and stubborn.)
- 'Waste not want not – you should never have thrown it away, we could have used it today.' (Pointing out a moral lesson and blaming the other person at the same time.)

In all of these, whether directed at a child or an adult, the speaker is trying to control someone. They use language and expressions that hurt, taking no account of the other's feelings and self-esteem. Their strongest message is that the speaker disapproves of the other. They address any less strongly the problems arising from the other's behaviour.

Let us take take another example, this time where the control message may seem less obvious. A member of staff in a nursery notices that a mother who is changing her young baby is not managing very well. She takes the nappy from the mother with a sigh and says, 'I showed you the easy way to do that this morning!' Here, by reminding the mother that she had been

'Controlling' messages can be destructive and hurtful

given a demonstration earlier, the worker 'puts the mother down'. An important part of the message is that the mother is inexperienced and rather silly. This sort of communication can only be harmful. First, it may damage the mother's self-confidence in looking after her baby. Second, it harms the relationship – which should be one of warmth and trust – between the mother and the member of staff. Yet parents and the people who work with their children – whether they are childminders or school nursery nurses, whether they work in a day nursery, a hospital, a playgroup or a kids' club – need to be cooperative and respectful of one another.

Disrespectful communications between colleagues, between staff and parents and, most important of all, between workers and children, are destructive.

Points to discuss or think about

In the example given above, the message from the nursery worker to the mother – that she is superior and the mother is inferior – is not hidden, and might also be conveyed to any onlookers, including the children. Nevertheless, she may be unaware of this and might protest, 'I only told her that I'd shown her this morning ... I didn't mean anything else by it.'

• Do you remember from your own experience any episodes where someone communicated, without saying it in so many words, that they were superior to someone else? What happened?
• Are there times in your work when you need to be especially careful not to communicate in this way?
• Which of the following pieces of advice would you give to a new member of staff (you are only allowed one): 'Try always to be tactful even if you don't feel like it' or, 'Always show respect to people because they're fellow human beings with feelings just like you'?

Observation

During the next few days, be on the look-out for anyone trying to control another person – adult or child – by using blaming or moralizing language. This could be in real life or on television. What happens?

Hidden and indirect messages

Some communications in nursery work contain harmful messages which are much more difficult to spot. Subtly, even unintentionally, they convey the idea that certain groups of people, parents and children, are different from the rest in important ways. Such hidden messages convey that some groups are not valued in the same way as others. The under-valued groups include people from minority ethnic communities compared with the rest, girls compared with boys and people with special needs, such as mentally or physically disabled people, compared with others. Because they are under-valued, and to maintain the power of more dominant groups, these groups do not have the same chances in life as other people – they are discriminated against and do not have equal opportunities.

Equality between social groups

In order to combat this injustice, many organizations involved in childcare and play, including voluntary organizations and local authorities, advise their members about good practice – ways of working which treat children with equality. This may include how families obtain places in childcare and play services and the type of service they receive. (You can obtain further information from the organizations listed at the end of this book.)

Also employers, including some local authorities and voluntary organizations, have employment policies which aim for equality. These cover, for example, how jobs are advertised and how people are selected for a post. The policy might also insist that records are kept and analysed about applicants' gender, ethnic background and whether or not they have a disability. This is done to monitor whether the advertisements are getting through to all sections of society. These are complex subjects and worth looking into; for example, you could make enquiries about the equal opportunity policies held by your employer or about any organization you might wish to work for, or read the titles listed at the back of the book.

In the rest of this chapter, we will look at messages of equality and inequality which can be conveyed, unintentionally perhaps, by people who work with children and their families. These also are *controlling* messages, but the control is less open and direct and perhaps more difficult to spot than the open control we examined at the beginning of the chapter.

Stereotyping leads to inequality

Hidden control messages are often contained in *stereotypes*. *Stereotyping* is when we do not see people as individuals, but are more concerned with them as members of a group, such as an age group, a profession, a racial group, whether they are men or women, boys or girls, gay or 'straight', able-bodied or disabled. When people use stereotypes they focus on characteristics which they believe are true of all the members of that group. Stereotyping can include statements about supposedly good points as well as bad ones. Here are some examples of stereotyping that you may notice in work with children:

'Black children are naturally good at music.'

You may be surprised that stereotypes can involve 'good' qualities as well as unpleasant ones. But if a play worker says, 'Black children are all born singers and they've got a natural sense of rhythm' then they are denying black children their essential individuality. Some black children are very musical, others are average and others not very good. Stereotyping is a way of lumping people together, ignoring ways in which they are different.

'Boys are more adventurous than girls.'

In fact, some girls are more daring than some boys. Some boys are not daring at all. By the things they say and do, workers can pass this attitude on to children, so that girls may not feel free to play with adventurous equipment. For example, at the annual general meeting of one playscheme, a report was accompanied by many slides showing boys swinging, climbing and being adventurous. The speaker made comments on the slides like, 'They're real lads, aren't they?' The photographs could have shown girls using the swings (because they *did* use them), but instead the speaker had, unconsciously, been controlled by a common stereotype and was reinforcing it for the audience. The indirect message was, 'This equipment is for boys.' The harm is done on two fronts: girls do not feel permitted to be adventurous and boys do not feel adequately 'male' if they prefer quieter pursuits.

'A mother's place is in the home.'

This old-fashioned saying is one of the ways in which women have been 'kept in their place'. For the sake of equality both mothers and fathers have important roles to play at work *and* at home.

'Asian girls are quiet.'

This stereotype may lead staff to pay less attention to Asian girls, because they do not expect any trouble from them. Also its use may suggest that 'quietness' is a good thing – although in some circumstances assertiveness or noisiness may be preferable.

'People with learning difficulties do not experience grief in the way other people do.'

There are many individual differences in how people experience bereavement – whether they have learning difficulties or not. It is unrealistic and disrespectful to deny a child (or adult) the experience of grief on the grounds that they cannot understand. It is always better to acknowledge people's sadness; not to do so implies that they are not fully human (see pages 51–2).

'The people round here don't really care about their kids.'

This stereotype writes off all the parents in a neighbourhood. It shows great disrespect and it must be inaccurate. Staff who use this sort of statement are claiming their own superiority and are probably out of touch with the lives and experiences of the families using their service. Even if what they say seems to be true of certain individuals, staff should ask themselves whether a parent's apparent lack of concern might, for example, be due to poverty, ill health or unemployment.

Like other controlling messages, stereotyping can be a powerful source of interference for the listener; that is, it can block or distort communication (see pages 43–5). Anyone who is aware of being stereotyped can feel angry and defensive, unprepared to listen. This is hardly surprising: the use of a stereotype shows that the speaker is only aware of the other as a member of a group, with its supposed characteristics. These characteristics may in themselves be offensive but, whether they are or not, the speaker shows that they do not see the other person as an individual. If the stereotyped person objects, they are often dismissed as 'having a chip on their shoulder'.

Stereotypes can also cause problems for those employing them. In work with children, stereotyping can distort how staff experience other people and can lead them to see and hear what they expect to see and hear rather than what is actually happening in front of them. This is to distort reality to match prejudices, a dangerous practice when the result is to keep people in their place, especially when this is a place of inequality. Critically it may deny some children access to a full range of resources intended for them to devlop skills and learn new ones.

When staff employ stereotypes, they are likely to encourage characteristics which fit in with the stereotypes, such as supporting boys in boisterous play and suggesting quieter occupations for girls. They may even excuse unacceptable behaviour; for example, boys may be permitted a certain amount of 'rough' behaviour that would be frowned on in girls. In addition, the stereotype that 'black boys can't concentrate' can lead to nursery staff accepting that the boys play less cooperatively and will commandeer, for example, tricycles and other wheeled outdoor toys. In this case, there will be less input from adults – the stereotype itself may be helping to create the stereotypical behaviour.

Children are thus moulded into ways of behaving which do not, in the long run, serve their best interests. They become limited in what they think of as appropriate behaviour: boys are not allowed to cry, appreciate beauty or express sensitive emotions; girls may not be assertive, use technical equipment or play football; black children may be encouraged towards musical or athletic activities but feel out of place taking part in other things. Children from minority ethnic groups may feel valued for whatever seems exotic about their culture, but not for everyday things.

The problem with stereotypes is that they serve to control people and keep them 'in their place'. The people who employ stereotypes may be quite unaware of this; they may have no idea that their communications contain hidden messages which exercise power and control over others.

Points to discuss or think about

- In your experience, is there much stereotyping to be found in work with children?
- In addition to those given above, can you think of any other 'positive' or seemingly harmless stereotypes?
- Can you remember any times when you have been stereotyped? How did you feel? What did you want to do?

Observation

During the coming week become aware of any stereotyping you come across. It could be at work, on television or elsewhere.

Social control

Very early in life children come to understand the value that society at large places on different groups of people.

Sexism

Sexism is one example of social control. It is the way in which women and girls are 'put in their place' by society at large and by institutions. In early years and play work, it can be seen in the way services are organized, how they are made available to the public and in their day-to-day practice. This is a wide area ranging from employment practice to language and behaviour, which is insulting towards females. Are both men and women employed in services so that they can provide children with positive role models – women who can play and men who can care? It includes all the ways in which girls are denied opportunities open to boys – including the very different messages boys and girls receive from their earliest days.

Much research shows how babies are prepared for their role in life according to their sex. From the beginning children come to know something about their social role – and that of other people. Boys as well as girls soon learn what is expected of mothers as much as of fathers. People treat even very little babies differently according to their sex (an example is given in 'Points to discuss or think about', below). People have different expectations of them and, as they grow older, boys and girls continue to be treated differently. It is important for staff in early years and play work to be aware of these differences, and to work out specific ways of dealing with them when they arise.

Aspects of organization also carry messages. In classrooms, and even in less formal settings, girls may be asked to line up on one side of a room and boys on the other. Registers can be split between boys and girls, rather than an alphabetic list of all the children attending. Boys and girls have been known to have separate games at a Christmas party. The staff organizing the children like this may say, 'This is how we have always done it ... it doesn't mean anything ... it is just a way of organizing the children.' However, the hidden message to the children in these practices is that differences based on sex are highly important. And so they are, but only in very special and biological contexts – unless we make them otherwise.

Points to discuss or think about

- What are the hidden control messages in these statements?

  Teacher: Will one of the boys carry the chairs?
  Childminder: Big boys don't cry.
  Play worker: She's a real little tom-boy!
  Teacher: Girls on that side, boys over here.
  Nursery officer: We're going to ask if any of the fathers could help put up the stalls and if the mothers could make a cake.
  Ward sister: We put boys in blue cots, girls in pink.

- * Here are some experiments carried out with babies:

  Fathers were shown their newborn children for the first time, in a cot, through a glass screen. The scientists running the experiment asked each man, after he had viewed his child, what his impressions were. Those with a little girl baby used typically feminine characteristics to describe her: she was pretty, sweet and so on. The boys' fathers, on the other hand, used much more active and masculine qualities to describe them.

  Many experiments have been carried out in which a baby is dressed 'unisex' and handed over for a few minutes to an adult. Sometimes 'it' is given a girl's name, sometimes a boy's name. On other occasions the adult is not told the baby's sex. Always, if the baby is thought to be a little girl, then the adults treat 'her' more gently and soothingly. If the child is thought to be a boy, then 'he' is played with in a more rumbustious manner.

Do you think that these experiments have anything to tell us about how 'feminine' and 'masculine' characteristics arise?

---

*See for example Rubin, J.Z. *et al.* 1974. The eye of the beholder: parents' view on sex of newborns. *American Journal of Orthopsychiatry* **44**; Seavey *et al.* 1975. Baby X: the effects of gender on adults' responses to infants. *Sex Roles* **1(2)**.

Racism

Racism means all the ways in which people from minority ethnic groups are treated less favourably and as less important than other people in society and therefore put at a disadvantage. Racism has a long history and it still exists today. Working against racism goes far beyond the interpersonal communications which are the subject of this book. In order to eradicate discrimination against minority ethnic groups, staff and management need to address racism directly, planning their approach and monitoring progress.

Managers should recruit and train workers from different backgrounds – representative of the locality – and develop ways to meet the needs of parents who do not speak English. Staff should learn what they can about the communities they work with – and be ready to accept that different cultures have different traditions. For example, they need to be aware that in some traditions it is not considered 'bad manners' to eat with the fingers, rather than a knife and fork. Telling a child off for this confuses her and is a slight to her family. At the same time other children who are not in this tradition may comment adversely. Staff need to think about how to tackle the contradictions in this situation: for example, what to say to the other children in order to maintain respect for everyone.

Avoiding racism and promoting equality requires a conscious effort on the part of staff and management. In some early years and play services, this is lacking and results in experiences which are alienating for children and parents alike. One four-year-old black child told her mother, 'I don't like very black people.' Other dark-skinned children may fantasize that their skin will turn white. At the same time, white children may come to believe that they are superior to the others. This is not only a matter of what happens in the play scheme or at the nursery, but these are the places where staff can have an effect on children's experiences. It means having ways of challenging insults – even in the nursery, children can be heard using racist insults – racist jokes and attacks. Many early years and play workers would be shocked at any suggestion that they treated some children unequally. But unless staff make a conscious effort, racism is difficult to avoid.

When you go into a play service, nursery or children's ward or visit a childminder, look out for the following:

- Are there play materials, books and toys to which all the children and parents can relate?
- What about the pictures in books, on walls and in jigsaw pictures? Can all the children find people to identify with? Are people from minority ethnic groups portrayed in a positive light or are they negative caricatures?

  Caricatures can create lasting and demeaning images for a child – white or black – to carry with them and can be damaging within the context of a racist society. Caricatures of white people are less damaging because the children will see positive images of them in many places.
- If there are dolls, is their skin colour, hair and dress representative

of children using the service? Again, are physical characteristics sensitively portrayed?

- Is brown 'flesh colour' paint mixed for the children, as well as beige 'flesh colour', so that they can easily portray people with different coloured skin? Is there brown plasticine for making people?
- Does dressing-up material include a good collection of clothes reflecting the different backgrounds of the children: for example, sari lengths, Rasta caps and black wigs? Are they well kept and do the staff know what different garments are called?
- Does the home corner have a choice of foods and cooking utensils? Again, do staff know the names which children use for these? If they do not, their communications with the children will be more difficult, or they will find themselves using expressions such as 'Indian bread', which covers a range of different types of bread. This carries the suggestion that the daily experience of children of minority ethnic groups is less important and interesting than that of the majority group. It is as though they are saying that a general term will do for many special types. In working with children, this sort of carelessness may diminish their pride in their own ethnicity.
- What about the major festivals celebrated in the local communities? Are there signs that any are celebrated with the children?
- Do 'interest tables' and other displays have pictures and objects that reflect the ethnic variety to be met in the local community?

If what you see reflects the local community, then there are messages for all the children present – not just those from minority ethnic groups. The message is that staff wish to treat all children and parents with respect, to help them to feel at home and welcomed. In this way staff set the atmosphere for children and families. Even if there are no children from minority ethnic groups present, pictures and toys representative of the wider society are interesting for the children who use a service. They also prepare them in a positive way for contact with people from other groups.

It must be stressed that this approach cannot be carried through without training and information. For example, it is disrespectful to attempt a special celebration without asking the advice of someone who has special knowledge – a parent or colleague – about what the celebration means and how it should be done. Community groups, the local Racial Equality Council and your Local Authority Education and Social Service advisers can also provide information.

In a nursery where staff had not got hold of relevant information they still wanted to do some 'multicultural' activities. Unfortunately, what they produced was more damaging than if they had done nothing at all. They got the children to make pointed cone-shaped hats to celebrate the Chinese New Year. Then staff led them in a procession in which the children took tiny steps, bowed from the waist to each other, and used pretend Chinese language. This produced a ridiculous stereotype which was insulting to Chinese people and was also likely to linger in the children's minds. It would have been much better if the staff had taken time to learn more about the festival they were 'celebrating', even if it had meant postponing the celebration for another year.

As well as learning about special events, it is important for staff to get to know about the everyday lives of the children they work with. One worker commented to a child playing at making tea in a home corner that she should not make it with hot milk. Yet it was the custom of the child's mother to prepare it in this way. The danger in this example is that the child could become confused, and her self-esteem and sense of identity could suffer. Over time she could develop the idea that the way things are done at home is not the 'proper' way, and not acceptable within the majority community. Yet the worker could have found out more about what the child was doing by discussing it with her. Just reflecting back (see pages 43–5), 'Now you are boiling the milk,' and then asking a question, 'Is that what your mummy does?' could have been enough.

The example also points to the desirability of staff becoming familiar with the customs and habits of all the ethnic groups who use their service and having an open attitude towards them.

Some nursery workers may object that anti-racism practice is not important in their work, because they work with babies, and babies, they believe, are too young to be affected by different ways of working. We know, however, that learning about who you are and your social relationship with others starts at a very early age. It is at the heart of work with children that they should grow up feeling confident and happy about their identity and that everything possible should be done, from the beginning, to encourage this. So pictures and toys in baby rooms, hospital wards and at childminders' homes should be chosen to present young children with positive images of themselves. At the same time, such pictures and toys will give parents some assurance that people of their ethnic group are welcome. This is one step towards achieving the cooperation and trust between parents and staff which is vital for the well-being of children.

Other people who work with children, of whatever age, may say something like, 'When I look at children I just don't see their colour. Children are children. I'm colour blind! I treat them all the same.' It may be true that a worker gives little consideration to skin colour or other indications that a child belongs to a minority ethnic group. But this is not the point. If people are to be socially equal, then it is sometimes necessary to treat them differently. It is necessary, for example, to bring in interpreters if staff do not speak the same language as a parent. Also a child's ethnicity and colour is an important part of their identity and should be acknowledged in equipment, activities and other practices.

It is especially important that children and their families should not be insulted by racist expressions and name-calling within any service for children. Nor should they be insulted by other people using racist body language – such as turning their back on another person. The approach to confronting someone who uses racist language is given in Chapter 11. Very clear *boundaries* (see pages 98–100) for adults and children should be set, because racist language is racist language, whether it is written or spoken, when it is used as a joke, when it is used by children who do not properly understand its meaning and when it is used by staff or by parents. Racist language is used to hurt and to diminish people. Although someone may excuse a child, saying, 'It's just a habit – he doesn't mean anything,' this is not the point. The child who is being racist is harmed if adults do not intervene: there is a lesson here that to be racist is to have an advantage and an easy weapon against others. Expressions which have an established racist meaning get through to their target. They are messages which are loaded with meaning about the 'superiority' and power that one social group has over another. They are also messages which help to maintain that power. So whether they are 'meant' or not, their use should always be challenged.

Equality for children with disability

Disabled children are a good example of how children should not always be treated the same in the name of equality. Disabled children have *special needs* in childcare and play services, as well as within the education system. So play workers and early years staff must do what they can to meet those needs, in many different ways. It goes without saying that there should be disability access, so that wheelchairs can get through doorways and into toilets. The use of expressions which are insulting to people with disabilities should always be challenged. There should also be positive images displayed – photographs and posters showing people with disability taking an active part in events. There are many specialist books which tell the stories of children with different conditions – hearing impairment, spina bifida and so on. All of these provide a focus for discussion between staff and children, giving children information and providing them with a language which they can use without embarrassment about the condition.

Communicating with a child's parents is even more important for a child with disability than for other children. Staff need details about the child's medication (if any) and their condition. Perhaps knowing the medical label for the condition is less important than having information about its effects. Parents should be asked, for example, about any limitations on the child's mobility; their mobility aids and how these are used (inexperienced workers can put a child in a walking frame the wrong way round); the protective clothing, such as a safety helmet, which a child wears at all times; any communication difficulties – does the child understand spoken language, even if they do not use it?; the signs or words a child uses to suggest that they want a drink or to go to the toilet; and their favourite activities. Is there any other important information about the child?

The children who are already in the setting should be prepared in advance for a child with disability. One way of doing this is by using the small dolls, known as *Persona* dolls, and telling their story. These dolls are intended for staff to use with children – they are not for children to play with themselves. They can not only be used for giving information about a child's disability, but also help children to understand and empathize with children who are poor, or children who have 'two mummies', or other children whose situation is unfamiliar in some other way. They can be used frequently for story sessions, too.

Some days before the new child's arrival, one of the dolls is described as having the same disability, for example, impaired hearing. Then the staff member describes a day in the life of the child: going to school, meeting friends and so on. All this is acted out with the doll. The storyteller points out the consequences of not being able to hear, but at the same time describes the child's ability to lip-read and use sign language (these details need to be checked with the new child's parents, in advance). The children are encouraged to imagine what it is like not to be able to hear, or they might be asked to cover their ears with their hands. The play worker also talks to the doll, positioning it directly in front of them 'where she can see', and speaking very distinctly. 'This is how to talk to our deaf friends,' the play worker says. Using these dolls can be a powerful way of building up children's capacity to understand another child's experience and point of view. The children might also be introduced to some sign language.

This sort of preparation, including using books and other methods, is one way to help children to communicate with one another. But a worker may also have to be ready to step in to help children to play together. It can be very easy for a disabled child to be left as a spectator, just watching other children, unless staff take positive steps to help them to join in. Some playschemes have devised group games which can involve all children. Others, which have a substantial proportion of children with special needs, have rules which say, for example, that computers or other equipment may not be used without a disabled child participating in the group.

As well as the risk of being mere spectators, disabled children may sometimes be treated by other children as having permission to be naughty. They can be encouraged to 'show off' and break rules for the other children's fun. Staff who see this happen should tell the children concerned that this is not fair and suggest other ways they can play together. At the same time they should communicate to the disabled child that a *boundary* has been ignored (see pages 98–100), and that the behaviour is not acceptable. It is condescending to allow a disabled child to do things which others are not allowed to do. It also gives a negative message about them to other children. Just as with other children, and in keeping with the child's ability to understand, reasons for finding behaviour unacceptable should be given. A firm, 'No, that hurts,' may be enough, or if necessary removing the child from whatever is causing problems. As with other children, if a disabled child's behaviour is frequently challenging, this needs to be discussed with parents who may be able to make suggestions. The local authority special needs advisor, or a specialist voluntary organization (see pages 124–5) may also be able to help.

Working with children with disabilities can be very rewarding. The children's parents should be told about such achievements as the children making new friends and acquiring new skills, so that they can take pleasure in them as well as the staff.

Exercise

In early years and play services, activities often centre on books. Sometimes these are used by individual children, at other times staff use them for story telling. Beware! Hidden messages about the value placed on different children are to be found in the book corner. These messages depend on how representative the books are of the children present, and on the pictures within them. If the books are varied and the pictures do not portray stereotypes, story sessions can help to communicate to the children that all people are valued equally. But even a skilled communicator and gifted storyteller would find it difficult to convey this message with books that were badly chosen.

- Find a children's book that you think would be popular with the children you work with. Go through the book and notice the part played by girls and the part played by boys in the first five pictures.

  Count how many men and boys there are compared with women and girls (if the book is about animals, very often it is clear if they are meant to be male or female).

  Is a girl or a boy in the foreground of the pictures? Is the person who is drawn biggest a girl or a boy in each picture? (See illustrations below.)

  Notice how often *male* characters are taking the lead, active, watching someone else do something, helping someone else.

  How often are the *female* characters taking the lead, active, watching someone else do something, helping someone else?
- Are there any books about people from *minority ethnic groups*? What proportion is there?

  In a book showing children from more than one ethnic group, repeat the exercise given above, but this time look at the different parts played by black people and white people.
- Are there any books about *children with disability*? What proportion is there?

If children are limited to books with pictures like these then the suggestion is that girls and women provide an audience for boys and men, that boys are active, that black children are athletic, that the family car is for the men in the family while women are usually involved with childcare, and that the normal family is white with two parents.

Repeat the exercise on page 85, this time taking children with disability as the subject. How usual is it to find a book containing positive images of children with disability?

When you have examined each book, decide if it contains any hidden messages about males and females and about people from ethnic minority backgrounds. Would it be a good book to use in the nursery? If other people have done this exercise, compare notes with them.

Points to discuss or think about

- You work in an inner-city school with children from different ethnic groups. It is Christmas and the teacher decides to put on a nativity play. She follows her usual practice: all the shepherds are played by boys, all the angels by girls; Mary is white, one of the three kings is black.
  Would you have any objections to the play?
  Why do you answer as you do?
- You confront a child about using a racist or sexist expression. She answers, 'But my dad says that.' What sort of things could you say to her which would protect other people, yet also respect her relationship with her father?
- What would you say to a child on a playscheme who was imitating a child with learning difficulties?

MESSAGES ABOUT POWER AND EQUALITY: KEY POINTS

- Many interpersonal communications contain messages about control. Some of these are quite open as one person exercises, or tries to exercise, power over another by insulting them or moralizing about their behaviour or putting them down in some other way.
- These controlling messages can be a source of interference in interpersonal communication because of the distracting emotions they arouse.
- Stereotypes can seek to control whole groups of people by suggesting what behaviour is expected and acceptable from them. This is a way of 'keeping people in their place' and contributes to sexism, racism and other unjust attitudes.
- Over and above any stereotyping, the toys, books and activities used in early years and play work can suggest the behaviour expected from black people, white people, able-bodied people, handicapped people, girls or boys.
- Treating people equally does not mean treating them all in exactly the same way.
- Not providing appropriate materials for all the children using a service suggests that some groups are less important than others by ignoring them and their experience.

10 Conflict: receiving criticism

Wherever you work, situations are bound to arise when you are directly involved in conflict arising from your work, when the subject matter of your communication will centre on differences or disagreements between yourself and others. There will be times when another person, perhaps your boss, perhaps a parent or an angry child, will be critical of something you have done and will tell you about it. On other occasions, you yourself may be critical of someone's behaviour and decide, for professional reasons, to talk to them about it.

People react differently to such situations depending on the circumstances, on who is involved and on their own particular temperament. But it is important to remember that interpersonal conflict does not necessarily have negative results: it can be a starting point from which people come to understand one another better, take more account of the other's point of view and find constructive solutions to their differences.

This chapter shows you how to make use of what you have learned so far about interpersonal communication in a particularly difficult circumstance: when you are at the receiving end of criticism. It aims to help you to work for a positive outcome when someone *confronts* you about something, that is, when they openly tell you that in some way or other you are causing them a problem. The criticism may be delivered with some tact or, on the other hand, the other person may not consider your feelings at all and be, in your eyes, quite offensive – they may use the blaming and moralizing approach discussed earlier.

Nobody likes being criticized, even when the criticism is justified. It can shake your confidence and leave you feeling upset and angry, especially if the criticism is expressed with hostility and aggression. Nevertheless, there are things you can do in the face of criticism which are constructive, rather than destructive, and which can help to build good relationships in your work.

There are five steps to be taken:

1 Keep cool: avoid escalation.
2 Listen: show you understand.
3 Apologize.
4 Put misunderstandings right.
5 Win/win situations.

1 Keep cool: avoid escalation

It is often easier to say 'keep cool' than to do it. However, keeping cool in the face of criticism may be absolutely necessary for the good of all concerned.

If someone has reached the point where they feel that they must do something about a difficult situation, where they feel they must confront someone else, feelings are probably already running high. These could complicate matters and make things worse. The person who has the complaint and who decides to voice it feels aggrieved but, in addition, they may also feel anxious about making the criticism. The person at the receiving end of the complaint is also likely to feel emotions rising. However, when a person is criticized during the course of their work, they have a responsibility to see that their feelings do not stand in the way of good professional practice. It is important to make sure that the situation does not escalate.

For example, a mother is angry because she thinks a nursery worker has taken her bronchitic child out on a cold, wet morning. She is nervous about approaching the worker and is feeling quite agitated. She summons up her courage and marches determinedly up to the worker and gives her a piece of her mind. The worker's immediate reaction is of panic, followed by anger that the mother should speak to her so 'rudely'.

If the worker allows her own feelings to become involved and shows them to the mother, the situation could blow up into something far worse – into a row – a situation containing so much interference (see pages 29–30) that neither side would really hear what the other had to say. The nursery worker would not be open to the mother's very real anxieties about her child and the mother would not hear any explanation which the worker might offer in the course of defending herself.

If someone criticizes you, justifiably or not, you need to be aware both of your own feelings and of those of the other person – you can tell much from their non-verbal signs, how they use their voice, their facial expressions and so on (see pages 8–15). They may look angry, raise their voice and perhaps wave their arms or gesticulate emphatically.

When you are confronted like this, whether the person criticizing you is an angry child or a senior colleague, you need to notice signs of agitation or anger arising in yourself. If you do not, you may communicate your agitation to the other person, causing the emotional temperature to rise still further.

In such cases, a conscious effort to calm down is useful. Some people follow the old custom of literally counting up to ten; this at least stops them from saying the first thing which comes into their head. Just telling yourself to keep calm can also help, but you may need to repeat it, to remind yourself more than once.

If the other person is very upset, you should make a decision about whether your conversation should happen 'here and now'. Is the entrance to the after-school club, with children standing listening, a suitable place for talking to a visibly angry parent? Should you allow a noisy confrontation to take place in a baby room? Would a 'cooling-off period' help? Is there any

A cooling-off period is going to be necessary before these two can start to work things out

way that you could postpone the interview, whether for five minutes or for a day or more, in order to take the heat out of the situation?

If you do try to obtain a cooling-off period, or wish to move the conversation to a more suitable location, be careful not to appear to be dismissive of the person or of their grievance. Explain that you are taking the complaint seriously, but that you could give it more careful consideration if you could talk about it in a quieter place or at a time when you could give it your full attention. Do not be vague about where and when you could meet to listen to what they have to say. Be specific about arranging a time and place which would suit both of you.

Exercise

Find as many ways as you can of saying, tactfully, that you would like to put off holding what looks like becoming a heated discussion until another time.

2 Listen: show you understand

The importance of listening carefully to criticism must be emphasized. Let the other person have their say without interrupting: hear them out. Then let them know that you understand the substance of their criticism by *reflecting back* what they have said (see Chapters 5 and 6). This is also a way of checking that you really *do* understand, because if you have misunderstood they will almost certainly put you right.

For example, a playscheme colleague comes and says, 'I'm really fed up with the way you always leave equipment out on a Wednesday afternoon so that I've got to put it away when I come in on a Thursday morning. It's not good enough. I've not got time to do your work as well as my own. Just because you leave early on Wednesdays doesn't mean you can't clear up. I can't clear up your things and get on with everything I've got to do at the same time. Anyhow it's not fair on the children.'

A reply that lets your colleague know that you have received the message would be the most useful first step. Something like, 'You've always got to clear up my stuff Thursday and you can't get on with your own work?' This reflects the content of the criticism: your colleague has to tidy up after you. Even if you say this, it is still possible that they will not realize that you have really heard them and may repeat some of their complaint: 'I've got enough to do on Thursdays, I can hardly manage as it is.' Reflect back again, including reflecting their feelings: 'Because I don't clear up last thing on Wednesday, you feel really pushed on Thursday morning.'

Any solution or explanation or apology you want to give may not be properly heard until the criticizer knows that you understand their point of view, that you are not avoiding it or denying it; in short, you are taking their complaint – their experience – seriously. In facing criticism, as in all interpersonal work, respecting the other person's experience is important.

3 Apologize

If you are in the wrong, apologize. Everyone makes mistakes, it is just part of everyday life. It could be that you have misunderstood or forgotten an instruction; or perhaps you had not realized how your actions would affect another person. In these circumstances the most realistic and respectful way forward is to acknowledge that the other person has cause for complaint. Say that you are sorry and, if appropriate, what steps you are going to take to put things right. In the example given in (2) above, you might reply, 'I'm sorry about the equipment, I thought that you'd want to use it, but I should have checked. I'll pack it away in future.'

4 Put misunderstandings right

In some cases all that is necessary is to put right any misunderstanding that underlies the criticism. So in the example given in (1) (above), where a mother is worried about her bronchitic child, there might have been a misunderstanding on the part of the mother. Having listened carefully, the best thing for the nursery worker to say would be something like, 'You thought

Carol went out to play, with her bad cough? I can understand why you're annoyed. But in fact she didn't go out at all. I've kept an eye on her all day.'

5 Win/win situations

If a situation cannot be resolved by a simple explanation or apology, then the most useful attitude in any conflict is that both sides should be satisfied if at all possible – you want the best outcome for everybody. So, first try to understand the other person's point of view and the reasonableness of it, and reflect this back. Then try to explain your own point of view (the next chapter goes into this in greater detail) and invite the other person to join you in finding a solution that suits both of you – even if there has to be some give and take. If you try to win at the expense of the other person, by putting them down in some way or stealing an advantage, you may find that both of you (and maybe other adults and children with whom you work) lose out.

For example, Steve, a nursery worker, comes to Nadina, in the next room, and complains that Nadina's group always has musical activities when his group is having a quiet time. At first Nadina is angry because Steve's manner is abrupt. But she keeps calm, listens to Steve's complaint and lets him know that she understands the problem and Steve's feelings about it.

Steve relaxes somewhat and Nadina explains that her group has music at that time because it is when it is their turn to have the nursery's musical instruments – but she's sorry for the disturbance. She asks Steve if they can think of any solutions between them. They think of all sorts of ways out of the problem including using different rooms and swapping round the times when different groups use the musical instruments. In the end they come up with an idea that suits both of them, to the benefit of both their groups.

Points to discuss or think about

- Can you remember times when having something out with someone – or their having it out with you – seemed to clear the air? Have there been other occasions when relationships have deteriorated after criticisms were made?
  Were there any differences in how matters were handled in these different cases?
- Which of the five ways of coping with criticism would you find most difficult: cooling the situation down; listening and showing that you understand the other person; apologizing; putting right misunderstandings; or finding a win/win solution? Do certain people find some ways more difficult than others?
- If a child criticizes a worker to their face, what should the worker do?

Practice

If any incident arises in which you are criticized, at work or elsewhere, use the skills you have learned about in the chapter. Later write notes about it – what happened, how you responded and the outcome. What was difficult? Were there any surprises?

Role play

There are two parts, Reg the father of Gary, aged two, and Sally his nursery worker. Reg found bite marks on Gary's leg yesterday evening and is very upset. He speaks to Sally about it first thing in the morning.

Try the role play twice: once with Sally being on the defensive and then with her trying to be as constructive as possible, in the ways suggested above.

What differences did you notice in Sally and in Reg in the two approaches?

CONFLICT: RECEIVING CRITICISM – KEY POINTS

If you find yourself at the receiving end of criticism or complaints at work, the following points can help you to be constructive, to the advantage of everyone concerned.

- If necessary, cool the situation down. Be aware of any interference caused by your own feelings and do what you can to keep calm. Notice the non-verbal communication of feelings coming from the other person.
- Try to see the other person's point of view and let them know that you understand. Reflect back what they say to you. This helps to clarify their complaint and shows that you are treating them with respect.
- Everyone makes mistakes sometimes, so apologize if you are in the wrong.
- If there is a misunderstanding, clear it up by explaining what has actually happened.
- Avoid a win/lose situation and use all your interpersonal skills to see that you both 'win'. Suggest that both of you think of all the different ways you can to get round the difficulty and together choose the one which is most mutually satisfactory.

11 Conflict: confronting another person

The last chapter was about the times at work when someone has a complaint and you find yourself at the receiving end of criticism. This chapter looks at the other side of the coin. It is about situations when you feel the need to *confront* another person – adult or child – about their actions. You decide that you should tell them directly about whatever is troubling you, in order to solve a problem.

For people who are not experienced in early years or play work, including students, it is often – though not always – better to consult a senior worker rather than approaching the person concerned directly. It would always be better to get advice if the matter was serious or if you were worried about what to do. Your place of work may have a policy about how to tackle certain problems, such as the use of racist or sexist language, parents being late or children's unacceptable behaviour. You need to find out about this if you do not already know. Also it may be that senior workers have information about a child or their family which needs to be taken into account. They may, therefore, decide that it is they who should take any action rather than leave it to someone who is inexperienced.

A decision to confront someone about a problem arising from their behaviour should only be taken for good professional reasons. A professional reason could be that the other person's actions are not in the best interest of the children, whether directly or indirectly. Or it might be that their behaviour has adverse consequences for you or your work. For example:

- In an under-fives playgroup a parent who comes in to help does not get involved with the children, but sits at the side all the time. You feel that her own child, and other children, miss out because of this.
- A colleague does something that seems thoughtless. Perhaps they chat for a long time on the telephone when there is a lot of preparation to do. This means that essential work is not completed on schedule, fellow members of staff are disgruntled and the activities which should be available for the children are not ready when they arrive.
- You are a childminder. A parent is frequently late picking up his child. You believe that the child becomes anxious when his father does not turn up on time. In addition, the father is breaking his agreement to collect his child punctually. This has an effect on your feelings – you feel resentful – and you cannot leave the house until he turns up.
- One child is aggressive towards another and uses racist insults towards him. You think that this is undesirable for both children.

In all of these cases you have a choice: either to put up with what is troubling you or to do something about it by confronting the person involved.

Although keeping quiet about a problem has its attractions – and no doubt you can think of cases where it is clearly the best course – there are also occasions when to do nothing would be a mistake, and you must take action. For example, staff working with children cannot stand by and allow them to hurt one another. But circumstances may not always seem so urgent and staff can put off confronting someone about a problem, even when they know it is necessary. This may be because they are afraid that the other person will react in an angry fashion. Or it may be because they feel over-protective and fear that challenging someone about their behaviour will be hurtful.

Whatever the reason, staff can bottle up their feelings with the result that their resentment may be shown in other, less direct, ways. Eventually, when they can put up with the situation no longer, they explode with anger and more damage is done than if the problem had been tackled earlier. The person under attack justifiably feels aggrieved and may say words to the effect of, 'Why didn't you tell me before? I didn't know I was causing problems.'

Clearly, it is better to confront 'unacceptable behaviour' earlier rather than later, so that it does not develop into an even larger problem. Do not behave as though someone else can read your mind – they need to be told if they are giving you concern. It is reassuring to realize that confrontation can be handled well – so that no one is unduly hurt and there is a satisfactory outcome.

But staff need also to think whether problems arise – including with children's behaviour – because of the way a service is organized. For example, there may be only one of a particularly popular piece of play equipment, such as a tricycle or a swing, which leads to competition and aggression among the children. This is a problem which staff must work to solve, asking themselves questions such as, how can we help the children to share things with one another generally, not just with this piece of equipment? Do we need more than one of these? Is there a fair way of organizing turns which everyone can agree about? Should we ask the children to put their minds to this as a group?

Points to discuss or think about

- Can you think of any situation which has deteriorated because someone has put off confronting another person about their behaviour?
- In your experience, are there occasions when it is better not to confront another person about behaviour which is causing you problems?
- Do staff always agree as to what is 'acceptable' or not? What problems can arise from this and what should be done about it?

How to confront constructively

Remember that you are confronting the other person about a problem which arises as a result of their behaviour. *You are not criticizing them as a person.* The outcome should be that the difficulty is overcome without damage to your relationship or the other person's self-esteem. This is always important – it is crucial in work with children.

Stay calm

Do not challenge anyone about their behaviour if you are feeling very agitated. Just as when you are yourself on the receiving end of criticism, you need to be sufficiently in control to be constructive and to chose your words carefully (see pages 88–9). If your feelings are not under control you may say things which undermine relationships and which you will regret later. Remember, a display of anger or annoyance can arouse feelings in the other person which interfere with how they receive your 'message'. There is a strong possibility that they will not really listen – they will be too taken up with their own feelings of anger, anxiety or shame, resulting from your unexpected 'attack'.

So remind yourself to stay calm.

Choose the right time and place

You have to decide when it is the right time and place for confronting someone about their behaviour (see pages 88–9). For example, in the heat of the moment, when you are feeling angry or hurt about something, you may not be able to confront a problem so that it has a good outcome. Or if a child has just hit another child, and is now throwing a tantrum, it is better to weather the storm and wait for them to calm down before you take any further action. Similarly, a time when an adult is obviously distressed about something is not a good time to bring up a problem.

Check misunderstandings

Once you have decided to confront someone, the first step is to check, politely and sincerely, that there is no misunderstanding on your part or that of the other person. This gives you the opportunity to back down gracefully if the mistake is your own, and the other person the chance to apologize if the mistake is theirs. For example:

Nursery nurse: Excuse me, did you know I'd just cut all that paper to take for Rainbow Room?
Teacher: Oh, I'm sorry, I thought it was for us.

Or you could check whether you understand the situation properly:

Play worker: Why did you throw all the dolls right across the room?
Child: Because there was a fire and they all ran away.

Nursery officer: Have I got it right, I thought you said Mary was going to help me on Fridays, but she thinks she should be in Sunshine Room?
Officer-in-charge: I'm so sorry, I'd forgotten to tell her. Or: No, if you remember that was for after Easter, when the new assistant comes.

Of course, in checking misunderstanding your non-verbal communication must back up the verbal communication. An accusing tone of voice could make the same words carry a very different meaning. Imagine the effect of, 'Excuse me, did you know I'd just cut all that paper to take for Rainbow room?' snarled between clenched teeth!

All confrontation needs tact and sensitive handling but some situations call for special care. Such a case is the example (above) of the playgroup mother who does not get at all involved with the children. You should check that she understands what she should be doing at the playgroup – it could be that she thinks she is there only to keep an eye on the children. Such a discussion would need some introduction, perhaps about how she enjoys being a helper or if there are any difficulties, rather than a bald question, 'How do you think you should be spending your time here?' Possibly she feels shy and you need to help her find her feet by encouraging her, rather than by confrontation.

Before continuing, you might like to try the following exercise.

Exercise

You could do this individually, in twos or as a whole group. In each of the examples below, imagine that you are the person who is speaking, confronting the other about a problem. Find other, more effective ways of challenging the other person. Suggest what you could say to open the conversation, checking if there is any misunderstanding on the part of the other person, or any difficulty that you do not know about.

- Ward sister to nursery nurse who is late for the fourth time in succession: 'You're very unpunctual!'
- Senior play worker to a student who is chatting in the staff room about some sensitive personal details disclosed to her by a child's mother: 'You're not supposed to gossip like that. It's not professional.'
- Nursery officer to a colleague who has opened a letter addressed to her: 'You've been reading my private correspondence!'
- Play worker to caretaker: 'Why is the floor in the hall wet? Why didn't you clean it earlier like you're supposed to? It's really dangerous, the children were slipping all over it ...'
- Member of staff to student putting toys away: 'That's really untidy.'
- One nursery officer to another: 'You've had our transistor for two weeks now. It's not fair.'
- Childminder to mother who comes late to pick up the children: 'It's really inconsiderate, coming late like this.'

- After-school worker to five year old who did not hang up his coat: 'You're really lazy today.'

Do not blame

If there are no misunderstandings between you, but the other person does not understand your problem, you need to help them to see things from your point of view. It will be difficult to achieve their cooperation, however, if you antagonize them. So in telling them about the problem do not blame them, or moralize about their behaviour, or comment on their character. Doing so is to show disrespect for the other person. It also causes interference (see pages 29–30), stops people from listening and, therefore, stops them from seeing your point of view.

If a member of staff says, 'Michael, you're a naughty, spiteful boy to bite Wayne,' perhaps the strongest message Michael gets is that the worker does not approve of him. It would be more worthwhile for the worker to help him to understand that Wayne has feelings and that Wayne is hurt.

Avoiding blaming language is vital, but it may not come naturally. Many of us are accustomed to situations where blame and criticism are used in order to control – or attempt to control – others (see pages 72–4).

Because blaming focuses on the person and not on the behaviour, it does not give clear information about the behaviour that is causing a problem.

Points to discuss or think about

Perhaps you can remember times when you have been at the receiving end of someone's criticisms and how you felt about it? In the episode below, see how many examples you can spot of moralizing and blaming. What effect is it having on Yusef, the nursery officer?

Jean, the deputy officer-in-charge, is just about coping today. The officer in charge is on leave and both nursery officers from the baby room have telephoned in to say that they are sick. Jean is the only nursery officer present who has any real experience looking after babies so she decides to cover the baby room herself, with Yusef, a newly appointed member of staff, from another room.

She is called to the telephone about an emergency admission. Before she goes, she asks Yusef to wash the bottle just used by the youngest baby and to bring the play pen and toys back in from the garden – it looks as though it is going to rain. Jean is away longer than she had hoped. She returns to find that Yusef has not washed the bottle nor brought the things in from the garden. As she thought, the rain is starting to fall. The food for the older babies will arrive in a minute, but nothing is ready. Yusef is just sitting there with one baby on his knee and one crawling on the mat in front of him. The others are in their cots. The following conversation takes place:

Jean: Look, Yusef, you've not done anything I asked you to. I expected you to get on so we'd be ready for the dinners when I got back. Instead I find you sitting there playing with the babies. You're just not pulling your weight.

Yusef: I thought ... I mean I couldn't do everything and Donna was crying and I thought I was supposed to ...

Jean: I asked you to do something and you just took no notice. You haven't even washed the bottle out. It's not good enough, you're supposed to be a trained nursery worker – I'd have been better off with a first-year student.

Yusef: (*sulkily*) I couldn't find the bottle brush and Donna started to cry so I picked her up ...

Jean: Look, here's the bottle brush, under your nose. Now for goodness' sake get on with it and try to get things ready by the time I come back.

'I' and 'you' language

Blame and criticism are often used to persuade people to change their behaviour, but they should be avoided. Instead, if you need to confront another person, tell them how their actions affect you and your work, including your responsibilities towards parents and children. Say what the matter is from your point of view: 'I feel ... I need ... I have a problem.' This is known as using 'I' language. The emphasis is on 'me', my responsibilities and needs, and the problems that arise for 'me' as a result of the other person's actions. 'You' language, on the other hand, puts the emphasis on criticizing and blaming the other person. 'You' language tells someone how awful, inconsiderate, untidy – or whatever – they are, and produces interference and hostility.

A useful formula for talking about how the other person's actions affect you is: 'When you ... I felt ...'. For example:

'When you were on the phone so long this morning, I felt really rushed and worried that I was not going to get everything done.'

Not:

'It's really inconsiderate leaving me to do all the work, while you waste time chatting to your friends on the phone.'

The first approach gives the other person information they might not have had before: that their actions put pressure on you. This in itself may be enough to bring about a change in their behaviour. It could also be an opportunity for them to tell you any good reason for the long telephone call. This positive way of dealing with problems clears the air and makes for good working relationships.

Setting boundaries

Sometimes a confrontation is necessary because of your professional responsibilities towards the people you work with concerning rules at work. These rules are often referred to as boundaries, marking the division between what is acceptable and what is not. Boundaries apply to the behaviour of both adults and children.

BOUNDARY-SETTING – CHILDREN

You sometimes need to let children know about boundaries, about what is acceptable and what is not. With a baby or toddler a firm 'No', accompanied by removing them from the scene of the 'crime' lets them know that you do not accept certain behaviour.

With an older child telling them about what is acceptable should be accompanied by the reasons why. Giving a child reasons can appeal to their own sense of fairness and shows that you take them seriously – they are not there just to obey orders without explanation.

If one child hits another you separate them and say to the aggressor, 'We don't hit other people – it hurts.' In this way you protect one child and give the other a clear understanding of what is expected. This makes for security; children know where they stand. You are also giving a reason for the rule and one which helps the child to remember that other people have feelings and rights, too. The same applies to the use of racist language. Children should be told that racist expressions are not acceptable because they hurt other people.

It may also be necessary to ask a child for explanations for unacceptable behaviour, that is, to clear up any misunderstandings (see pages 95–6) and to provide more information about the child's point of view. It is better to use a non-threatening question such as, 'What happened?' rather than 'Why did you do that?'

Sometimes a child may act against their own best interests, rather than harming someone else. For example, a child may do something which is dangerous. In play services for older children someone may persist in using craft equipment in a dangerous way, contrary to your instructions. Or a play worker may find a child smoking. Again the boundaries should be made clear, because children need to be protected from the results of their own dangerous behaviour.

In some play services and kids' clubs, children have meetings in which they suggest rules which set the boundaries for what is acceptable and what is not. These can then be referred to in order to settle disputes as something which has been agreed by everyone. For example, signing up for table tennis and snooker makes sure that everyone has a turn.

All of the above suggests that boundary setting should be accompanied with an explanation and an appeal to children's sense of fairness. However, this approach is not always taken and it has been known for staff to take more punitive measures, such as shouting at children, making them sit in the corner or even handling them roughly.* These are powerful communications, messages which tell children that 'might is right'. They ignore children's

*See *Play and Care out of School*, Pat Petrie (1994)

own developing sense of justice and their growing ability to reason. They can also damage a child's self-esteem, rather than build it up. Helping children to feel good about themselves is an important aim in early years and play work.

Points to discuss or think about

- 'I think you should tell children off if they do something wrong like hurt someone else or take their things. You should tell them that they're naughty.'

What do you think of this opinion?

- Is there any difference between a member of staff telling a child off and a mother doing it?

BOUNDARY–SETTING – ADULTS

Here is an example of a confrontation with an adult which involves setting boundaries. You are in charge of a childminders' drop-in centre; a new minder smokes while she is looking after the children – and local authority policy is against this. Clearly it is your responsibility to see that this does not happen and so you must speak to her about it. In the first place you should check that she knows about the rule and make the boundaries clear: 'Did you know we've got a no-smoking rule, when the children are here?' This gives her information which she might not already have; it also gives her the chance to back down gracefully.

If she persists you need to tell her where you stand and what your responsibilities are, using 'I' language: 'I have to see that the no-smoking policy is carried out' ... 'I feel that it's best not to smoke in front of children because of the example.' 'It worries me when I see toddlers near lighted cigarettes,' or, 'I'm concerned for the children's health.'

It is important to show that you understand her point of view and the effects this rule is going to have for her. For example, that you are sorry for any consequences of your action: 'I'm sorry you're missing your cigarette.'

But it is not helpful to apologize for asking her to keep to the rules – setting and maintaining boundaries is part of your job. So saying, 'I'm sorry I've got to ask you to stop smoking' is just not appropriate; in fact, it may not even be sincere.

Points to discuss or think about

What is the difference between saying that you are sorry for any consequence of asking a person to keep to the rules, and saying you are sorry about imposing a rule? Could you make up some more examples of these, based on your own work?

Think of solutions – problem-solving

As we saw earlier (see page 9), when there is conflict you should try to be creative: find ways out that satisfy both sides – 'win/win' solutions – and involve the other person in finding them. Invite them directly to think of ways round the problem: 'You want to smoke but I am not allowed to permit smoking here. Can we come up with anything to solve the problem?'

In the example above the minder could go into the next room for a smoke while you played with the children. But, again, there could be difficulties with this solution. Would the children be happy? Do you have conflicting duties that mean you have not got time to give the children proper attention? In the course of problem-solving, people may need to suggest several ideas before you find something mutually acceptable.

PROBLEM-SOLVING WITH CHILDREN

It is also possible to use problem-solving with children once they are old enough to understand the approach. If a child is going against the interests of other people, point out that this behaviour is not permitted, that is, set the boundaries (see pages 98–100) and briefly give the reason, for example, 'We don't hit other people, because it hurts them.' Then ask for the child's reason for what occurred:

'What happened?'
'She's got my car and I want it.'

Next involve the child in suggesting other ways of obtaining the required result: 'What else could you have done to get your car back?' Children soon get used to this approach and come up with ideas for themselves. You are helping them to be creative and to realize that they have choices about their own behaviour. They also learn that there are socially acceptable ways of solving their own problems.

Role play

You may be able to think of times when you wanted to confront someone but were nervous of doing so. Choose one such occasion for a role play. Do it twice, the first time ignoring the advice given in this chapter. The second time handle the confrontation as constructively as possible.

How did it feel, each time, from the point of view of the confronter and the confronted? What did the onlookers notice?

Exercises

Here is an opportunity to practise confronting problems so that you can do it effectively should the occasion arise. Choose a partner and confront each other about the difficulties described below. Each take a turn at both parts. After each confrontation talk about how you both felt – was it a successful confrontation from your point of view? What further possibilities can you think of about approaching the other person and solving the problem?

- A mother confronts a childminder because her child was not properly wrapped up to go out on a cold day.
- A nursery worker confronts a mother who continually forgets to bring back clothing – pants and tights – lent when the child wet herself at nursery. The nursery is short of spares.
- A play worker confronts another worker about always taking too long a coffee break.

Observation

During the next week or so observe confrontations as they occur around you, for example, at work, in a shop or on television. Include confrontations between adults and between adults and children. How do both parties react? Are the confrontations handled well?

Check what happens against the key points, given below, and decide what has the most effect on the outcome of the confrontation – whether this is positive or negative.

CONFLICT: CONFRONTING ANOTHER PERSON – KEY POINTS

- Sometimes it is professionally necessary to confront other people, adults and children, about their behaviour. If someone is acting against the children's interests, either directly or otherwise, then you should speak to them about it and ask them to change.
- Challenge the problem, not the person. Do not blame, moralize or tell off.
- Do not confront a child or an adult in such a way as to lower their self-esteem.
- When you confront, stay calm in order to avoid interference (see pages 29–30).
- Use 'I' language, explaining how you are affected by the other's actions.

12 Communicating in groups and meetings

Being in a group of some sort is a familiar experience for everyone. From childhood we have all belonged to many different groups. We start off in a particular type of group, the family, with parents or carers and perhaps brothers and sisters and other relatives. At an early age some of us go to nurseries and learn to be part of a group of children. We all went to school, where we were members of class and peer groups. In our free time, we may have attended play services and taken part in varied group activities, or we may have participated in Guides and Scouts or youth groups organized by different religious faiths. In adult life, most people have experience of working with a group of colleagues and may also be members of formal and informal groups in their leisure time.

The subject of this chapter is a certain sort of group: face-to-face groups in which you participate in your professional work. The aim of these groups is to create cooperation and communication and they may involve children, parents and/or staff. Whether groups meet only once or are a regular feature of the timetable, they are often brought together to draw on the experience, energy and skills of many people.

In early years and play work, groups serve a variety of purposes. A children's meeting at a play centre gives the children the opportunity to be heard on any current problems, or to contribute to plans for activities and outings. Sometimes parents and staff meet together to talk about mutual interests and concerns. In many children's services, regular staff meetings are called to plan and review the programme, to iron out difficulties and to exchange necessary information.

A group meeting can be a means of bringing out the best in people, because it can encourage its members to be creative in ways that would not have occurred to them as individuals. Groups also give their members an opportunity to experience that there may be many perspectives on life and work, as well as their own. But groups do not always function well. If they are managed badly or if people do not take a proper responsibility for playing their part as best they can, groups can be boring, frustrating and even destructive. People who have had unsatisfactory experiences in groups may feel very reluctant to attend or be responsible for what they see as 'yet another meeting'.

Groups need careful attention if they are to get off to a good start and they need commitment to keep them functioning well. What follows is some practical information about group work, and there is advice on how to make your own best contribution as a group member. The chapter also covers bringing together and leading different sorts of groups, so that they fulfil their potential by drawing on the talents and experience that different members have to offer.

Types of group

There are different sorts of groups for different tasks, and different types of group leadership. Broadly speaking, these may be reduced to three different types.

A directed group

A directed group is not the main subject of this chapter, but it is included because it provides a useful contrast with the two types of group described later.

A highly experienced person may call on a group of other people to work under their direction. For example, in a crisis a person with particular skills and knowledge may direct others. If there is a traffic accident involving several people, a qualified first aider may take charge and tell others what to do – asking someone to telephone for medical and police help, saying who may be moved, asking someone to find coats to cover anyone in shock, looking after those who need urgent attention. They explain what is to be done and exactly how to do it, check that instructions have been carried out and correct mistakes. The others accept this type of leadership because they recognize that expertise is necessary if lives are to be saved and no time is to be wasted. They may be highly creative people, full of ideas, but they are ready to put these to one side in these circumstances.

The same sort of directive leadership may be acceptable in other, less extreme, situations: for example, when a group of volunteers comes together to refurbish a nursery under the direction of a professional painter and decorator. The volunteers recognize the leader's expertise and get on with the job as instructed. They prefer it, of course, if the leader explains clearly, is good humoured and makes some allowance for their mistakes.

Points to discuss or think about

Have you had any experience of belonging to a directed group, such as those described above? How did you feel about it? What, if any, were the advantages and disadvantages? Have you ever felt that this type of leadership was used inappropriately?

A facilitated group for sharing experience or mutual support

The work of a group leader is not necessarily to instruct, supervise or organize. This sort of leadership would be inappropriate for a group where people come together for mutual support or to share their experience. For example:

- a group of parents who meet regularly to talk about bringing up children;
- colleagues who meet to discuss any difficulties they are having at work;
- children who are consulted about what they want from a playscheme.

In groups like these, an effective leader sets out to provide the conditions in which members may feel at ease so that they are able both to make a contribution, and be attentive to other people. In such groups, the leader is a facilitator, making the group process run smoothly but not directing the group members. Facilitators are not necessarily expert in the subject matter that is raised. They may facilitate a parents' group or a staff group, without themselves being parents or early years workers, or knowing at first hand the problems which members discuss. In this sort of group, the members' task is to share experience; the facilitator's is to see that this can happen.

If group members are not accustomed to a facilitated group, and are more used to being directed by an expert (as in the groups described above), they may feel confused at the way the facilitator treats the group and may want to call on them to provide 'right answers', or to side with one group member as being 'correct' compared with another.

There is nothing wrong in setting out to give information and there is often a place for straightforward teaching. Staff may enjoy a talk about play services or childcare in other countries, for example. Or parents might ask for a meeting at which an expert talks about adolescent development. But these are not tasks for someone acting as a facilitator with a group which comes together for mutual support. Here the opportunity to talk and to listen to other group members is what is required and it is the facilitator's responsibility to see that it can happen. It is important that new members understand that this is the nature of the group they are joining, otherwise they may become frustrated and angry.

The 'collaborative group'

Quite a different sort of group from those above is a working group which makes decisions or carries out a task. Individuals volunteer or are invited to join such a group because they have some particular experience or skill to offer. This group collaborates, or works together, on a task. For example:

- A management committee engaged in recruiting new staff and making decisions about the person specification, the level of pay, advertizing the vacancy, how to shortlist candidates and who is to be involved in interviewing.

- An informal working party, composed of staff and parents, deciding how to let local people know about their summer festival, whether by leaflet, informing schools, putting up posters or whatever. They would also decide who was going to carry out the different tasks involved, if any others should be included in producing publicity material, and whether and when to hold further meetings.
- A regular staff meeting in a service such as an adventure playground or a nursery.

In these cases the group leader would have the role of chairperson. Like a facilitator, the person who chairs a collaborative group has the job of making sure that the best contribution can be made by every group member. There is no point in having expertise within the group if it cannot come to the surface and be of use. Some group members are very knowledgeable and can be turned to for information; others may have artistic or organizational talents; still others see ways of reconciling different points of view and suggesting ways forward if a group gets stuck.

In a collaborative group, decisions are made about a task. The chairperson has to keep this task in mind, be ready to remind the group about it and move them forward when necessary. It is also the chairperson's work to see that all decisions and their outcomes are reviewed at the next meeting.

As you can see, the members and leaders of different sorts of groups have different functions. Leaders who act as experts and organizers have (in reality or in their imagination) all or most of the knowledge and skills required. They know what should be done and how to do it. They just need a work team to carry out their directions. They see that work is carried out properly and that group members do what they are told.

In support groups, facilitators concentrate their attention on the group, its members and their experience. In these groups, there are no decisions to be made about work, or about any outside goals; the members' contributions are valuable in themselves.

In collaborative groups, the joint attention of the chairperson and of group members is, or should be, on the task in hand. Together they want to achieve a certain goal, using all the expertise that is in the group.

Although it is possible to talk about these three different sorts of groups in theory, in real life they can sometimes overlap. For example, members of a directed work team may sometimes be asked for their ideas. A parents' support group may have to make decisions about a party or other event they want to organize. If this happens, depending on how complicated the event is, they may need someone to act as chairperson.

Being a group member

The following outlines how you can be an effective member of sharing and collaborative groups.

Responsibility for yourself

If you choose to belong to a support group or to a collaborative group, then you are responsible for your contribution to that group. (In a directed group some of this responsibility lies with the individual, but the leader also decides how the members are to make their contribution.) You may find speaking in a group easy or difficult; individuals are different – and that includes how they behave in groups.

It may be useful to compare group members to different sorts of animals, to show the variety that is to be met. Some people are like nervous gazelles, who allow other people to glimpse them, briefly, before darting swiftly away. Others are like the tortoise which slowly and certainly makes progress. Still others are like playful puppies: they jump right in, making quite a lot of noise, and enjoy themselves enormously; while some, like the owl, stay silent for long periods, before swooping down on their prey.

MAKING AN EFFECTIVE CONTRIBUTION

Here are some points which can help you to make an effective contribution, whatever your personality:

- If you have something to say, say it. This means being persistent and making sure that you are noticed by the rest of the group. So speak up clearly, as soon as another person stops speaking. In a more formal group, signal to the chairperson that you wish to speak next by raising your hand.
- Say what you have to say as plainly as possible and use concrete examples. Avoid jargon and unnecessary theory – they do not help people to understand what you mean.
- Be aware of your own feelings – are you feeling elated, anxious, sad, angry, bored? These could affect how you contribute to the group. Being aware will help you to express yourself without your feelings getting in the way.
- Be willing to talk about your feelings, as well as about your ideas. Say, 'I feel depressed when parents don't come to our evening meetings,' rather than, 'The trouble is that in this society there is an apathetic minority.'
- Do not hog the meeting, let other people in.

Responding to other people

As well as taking some responsibility for what you say, you need also to be sensitive towards other group members. The first part of this book describes how to listen in an encouraging way, being aware of other people's feelings and responding to them, and asking questions. It also talks about playing a positive part when conflict arises. All of this applies in a group as well as in encounters between individuals.

It is not the responsibility of the group leader alone to encourage everyone to speak and to affirm contributions – all the group members should play a role in this. Especially important is to address other group members, not just the group leader (except, that is, in a very formal chaired meeting). This can get ideas flowing between group members. It also helps the flow of the meeting if you refer to what others have said when you take your turn to speak. In doing so you build on other people's contributions. In addition:

- Be aware of other people's feelings. These are usually conveyed in their non-verbal behaviour, more than by what they actually say.
- Be prepared to confront other individuals, or the group as a whole, if you think that this is appropriate.
- Accept other people's talents, their experience and their willingness to take the lead during a meeting. In fact, be happy at the richness that is available and the potential it provides for an effective group.

Being sensitive to the group

Just as individuals are different, so are groups. Some groups are warm and trusting, others are rather cool and individuals do not communicate easily. There are groups which work enthusiastically; others find ways of avoiding whatever they set out to do, whether it is mutual support or fund-raising.

Here are some of the ways groups procrastinate:

- They spend a lot of time analysing and talking round the subject, without getting down to practical matters. For example, a planning group might talk at length about local politics, but not choose someone to book a venue so that a fund-raising event can take place.
- People generalize – they refuse to be specific. For example, they do not talk about their own experience but say things like, 'Sometimes young nursery workers can lack confidence in how they treat the children,' rather than, 'I didn't feel at all confident handling babies when I started in the nursery. Come to think of it I still feel happier with the older children.' Or, 'In the inner city people are often isolated,' rather than, 'Some of the mothers have told me they feel quite lonely and find it hard to make friends in the neighbourhood.'
- They treat subjects flippantly or make jokes when it is not appropriate. This may discourage group members who are afraid of not being taken seriously.

- They get sidetracked onto subjects which are not to the point.
- They may allow one or two people to talk about their problems most of the time. This ignores other people's needs, the contributions they could make and the work that is to be done.
- They spend their time arguing.
- They may find a scapegoat for their own failures. They may blame outside circumstances or a particular group member for what has gone wrong, rather than take group responsibility for any lack of progress.

If any of the above happen, the group is wasting its time and avoiding its main task. It is the responsibility of any member who notices this to confront the group about it (see pages 93–9). It is not the responsibility of the leaders alone.

Points to discuss or think about

- Think about how you behave in meetings. What sort of creature would you compare yourself with?
- Have you had any experience of a successful group – one which fulfilled its purpose? What sort of contributions from group members helped this?
- Have you ever been in an unsuccessful group – one which did not fulfil its purpose? Can you identify any of the ways in which it avoided its task? Were they similar to those listed above?

Starting a group

It is quite likely that, at some time during your career, you will decide to start a group related to your work. It could be a support group for parents, or perhaps one for volunteers. Or you might want a group of people to collaborate on a specific task, such as planning a programme of in-service training to meet their own working needs.

First you need to find members. If this is to be a group of colleagues then asking for volunteers may be enough. However, if you want to attract parents or other members of the community to join a group, personal contact is one way of getting started. You need to identify two or three people who would seem to be likely members and ask them if they would like to join you in setting up a group. Talk over your ideas about the group and then each invite others to come to a first meeting. It is important at this stage to remember the points made at the beginning of the book, about including different sorts of people and going out of your way to make sure the group is as open and welcoming as possible.

Let the wider community know that you are holding your first meeting by putting a notice in a newsletter, or on a notice board, with a name and telephone number for enquiries. Write a short, clear statement about the group's purpose.

Size of group

For a support group, about 12 people seems to work well. The group will be small enough for everyone to make their contribution and large enough to provide a mixture of experience and ideas. (For a parents' meeting, consider whether to provide childcare so that more parents would be free to attend.)

In a collaborative group, size depends on the overall task to be carried out, the time it has available to carry out the task and the amount of detailed work that is needed.

Meeting place

The room you meet in should be reasonably comfortable, so that people feel at ease and are not distracted by such things as hard chairs, draughts or noise.

There should be an understanding that other people will not come in and out during the meeting. This is especially important for a support group. The meeting place should be for that group only for the course of their meeting, otherwise it is difficult to achieve an atmosphere of trust and it is difficult to concentrate.

The meeting room should not be so large that the group is like a small island in the middle of a sea of space. This is intimidating and makes communicating with others difficult. If you have to use a large hall, think about making one half into your meeting place, using, for example, a screen to divide up the space.

Seating

Arrange the seating so that everyone can see everyone else and so can communicate easily with each other. Placing the chairs in a circle is the easiest way to achieve this, and is a way of indicating that everyone in the group is of equal value. Always try to avoid a chair outside the circle – a shy person sitting outside the circle will find it difficult to make a contribution.

Putting chairs in rows, with a leader facing the group, suggests that there is one expert and others who need to learn from them. This is not appropriate for these types of groups, although it may be acceptable in, for example, some types of training situations.

The first meeting

Prepare your own programme for the first meeting, with a welcome and a short statement about why you have invited people to come.

Make sure that people have an opportunity to be introduced and to get to know one another. Even if you know everyone present, it is possible that they do not all know one another. One way of doing this is to invite them to introduce themselves around the circle, or to ask them to stand up, walk around and find people they do not already know and introduce themselves.

The next thing to do is to help people to be clear about what they want out of the group and why they have come. This can be done by talking to each other in pairs. Ask people to choose a partner they do not know very well. This not only helps to break the ice, but also allows group members to get to know another person better. Ask them to interview each other, finding out: who they are, why they have come, what they are hoping for and if they feel any uneasiness about the meeting. Tell them they can have about five minutes each. Then in the whole group let each person introduce their partner to the others and say what their partner wants from the group. All the different expectations will then be out into the open.

Come to an agreement about what is a realistic goal for the group – you may want to write it down on a large piece of paper and then display it in front of the group. Also decide about how the meetings are to be run: will you have one leader or will you take it in turns to lead? How many meetings do you think you will need? Where will they be held and when? How long will each meeting last? Knowing these details in advance helps people to feel confident about the group.

Being a leader

You may be chosen to lead a group for several meetings or you may take turns with others.

As a leader (whether facilitator or chairperson) it is your job to be of service to the group and to see that it fulfils its purpose. Good leaders let the group have a life of its own. They do not make decisions for the group, but let decisions come from the group. They do not talk too much but they are always alert and observant. They try to be aware of the group atmosphere and of the feelings of individual members. They are in touch with whether the group is fulfilling its purpose or not, and can bring this out for the group. Leading a group is not always easy, but drawing on your own interpersonal skills helps, as does experience.

Let the group's purpose be clear. You need to help the group to be aware of what its purpose is by reminding them of earlier agreements. At some point they may need to clarify their purpose again. Members may ask for this, directly or otherwise. For example, you may notice that different group members seem to have somewhat different ideas about the group's aim. Or someone may say something like, 'What is this meeting about? I think we're missing the point.' If this happens you may need to spend a little time to clarify and agree on the group's purpose. Beware, however, that continual talking about aims may be just a way of avoiding the real work of the group.

Providing a structure for the meeting

People can feel insecure if they do not know how a session will be structured, so always introduce the subject of the meeting and say how it is going to be approached.

- In the case of support groups, agree in advance that whatever is spoken about in the meeting will be confidential and not raised outside the group. (If any problems arise because of this, for example, if you learn something which suggests that a child may be in real danger, follow the advice given on pages 118–19.)
- You may be using discussion material from outside the group which will have its own structure, so you may need to adapt it for the group's own needs. Are all the discussion points appropriate? Is there enough material ... or too much?
- If you are supplying the material for the meeting yourself, say briefly what you are going to do. For example, 'I thought it would be a good idea if we each looked through these cuttings I've taken from the local paper, and choose one that seems of most concern to you as a parent. This could start our discussion on children's play needs in this town.' You would also need to have ready some questions which could encourage people to share their experience and insights with each other. Open questions are more useful than closed questions to achieve this (see page 63).
- The group may need to reach decisions about a task which it has undertaken to plan and carry out. The decisions should be outlined as an introduction to the meeting: 'We need to choose a volunteer to represent us on the community council and we need to outline the most important things for them to say on our behalf.' If there are many decisions to be made, then a written agenda – either as a handout or written up on a large sheet of paper – will keep everybody informed about what is to be done.
- As leader, it is also your job to assist the group in deciding whether they want to follow any 'sidetrack' which is beginning to take up group time. This might mean leaving the agreed subject of the meeting for a later date. Unless a group actually makes a decision about this, for or against, problems may arise and members may feel frustrated. If the 'sidetrack' is lengthy, they may not achieve what they set out to achieve by the end of the meeting. On the other hand, if the new material is not discussed, some group members may believe that unforeseen and important issues have been ignored. So let the group come to their own decision about this. Point out any implications such as the need to include the new subject on a future agenda, or the fact that the earlier subject may need to be dealt with at a later date.
- Sum up for the group at the end of a session. Remind them of any decisions taken, or briefly acknowledge the explorations and discoveries that have been made.
- Set the date for the next meeting.
- Be the timekeeper for the meeting and see that it begins and ends

promptly. This is most important. If meetings start late, work may not get done and people may come later and later for each meeting. At the end of a meeting, people who are kept beyond a stated time may be distracted, thinking of their other commitments (such as getting back for a baby-sitter) or they may have to leave early and miss information (such as the date of the next meeting). Keeping to the agreed time can help people to feel secure in a group.

Helping to keep communication flowing

- As leader, listen carefully to each person's contribution.
- Check if other group members have understood a contribution if it seems to you that people look puzzled.
- Clarify any misunderstandings.
- Encourage people who have difficulty in expressing their thoughts or feelings, by reflecting back (see pages 43–4).
- Notice if someone is trying to get into the discussion and help them to do so by saying, 'Leroy, you wanted to say something ...'
- Help people to work through disagreements, aiming at solutions which are good for both sides (see page 91).
- Bring up new points or ask open questions (see pages 62–3) if the group needs to be moved along.

Closing a group down

It is sometimes necessary for groups to decide if they want to carry on in the same way or discontinue. It is not healthy to carry on if people are becoming dispirited and confused or if their work is finished. There are various options available.

When members move away, or leave for other reasons, the group can decide to recruit new people. They should realize, however, that new members will bring different resources, experiences and needs. If there are many new members, it will probably be necessary to work on a restatement of the group's purpose, together.

Sometimes people feel that their original purpose has been achieved and in this case they should decide if they want to take on new goals.

If people are no longer sure why they are meeting, they need to take time to look at their original purpose and to decide if they want to move on from it or to return to it.

It is also possible to decide that the group has come to the end of its useful life and that no purpose is served by continuing. If this is so, then farewells should be said, either quietly or with a party!

COMMUNICATING IN GROUPS AND MEETINGS: KEY POINTS

- At best, groups can encourage creativity and pool skills and experience.
- Each member of a group should take responsibility for its effective functioning – it is not just the business of the leader.
- There are different sorts of groups for different tasks, and different types of group leadership. Leaders who are seen as experts direct a work team. In mutual support groups, facilitators help members to define and explore their own interests. In collaborative working groups, the joint attention of the chairperson and of group members is, or should be, on carrying out agreed tasks, using all the expertise which is in the group.
- Members of sharing and collaborative groups should be responsible for making whatever contribution is in their power. They should use concrete examples and avoid jargon and unnecessary theory. They should be aware of their feelings and be willing, on occasion, to express them.
- They should be sensitive towards other group members, let them into the discussion and encourage their communications. They should also be prepared to confront other individuals if necessary.
- There are many ways in which groups fail to carry out their task. Some groups get sidetracked on to subjects which are not to the point, or a scapegoat may be blamed for group failures. Avoiding responsibility should always be confronted by any group member who is aware of it.
- Starting a new group means making decisions about publicity, group size and a comfortable meeting place which is likely to be undisturbed. The purpose of the proposed group should be made clear.
- A group leader should take care to introduce group members to each other, facilitate members' contributions and keep the group on task.
- A time comes when a group should either end or redefine its purpose.

13 Confidentiality

Although confidentiality is the last subject of *Communicating with Children and Adults*, it is not the least important. It covers those aspects of confidentiality that you are likely to come across in your dealings with adults and children in early years and play work. The chapter is about how you treat information which is disclosed to you (see page 57), whether as an individual or in the course of a group meeting, and whether you pass it on to any one else or not. It does not cover subjects such as storing sensitive written information or who has access to written or computerized records. These are important but they do not come under the heading of interpersonal communications. Private information can be passed on to you in different ways. Here are two of them:

- parents confide in you; and
- senior staff pass on private information.

In the course of your work, especially if you get on well with people, you will find that parents confide in you and tell you about their worries and problems. This may be because they like you and find you trustworthy, which is quite likely to happen if you treat them with sensitivity and respect. But, quite apart from their feelings about you, they may also need to confide in you just because of the job you do. They confide in you first and foremost because you are a professional working with their child. They might tell you private family details so that you can understand their child better.

For example, you tell a father, when he comes to pick up his toddler, that she is not her usual self; she is being a bit whiny and clinging. He explains that her mother is suffering from depression and has been taken into hospital. He did not tell you earlier because, he says, 'People can be funny about mental illness.'

This father would of course expect you to treat what he has told you as confidential. He has let you know about his problem because you work with his child, and need to understand her. He would not have told you otherwise.

Senior staff may also give you private information about families – not because it is interesting but so that you can do your job properly. For example, there are worries about Cathie, a child who has been physically abused at home and is on the non-accidental injury register. The officer-in-charge of a nursery passes on this information to the staff working directly with her. This is necessary because it helps to explain some of Cathie's behaviour and

Gossiping is unprofessional: it does not respect people's right to keep personal matters private

because, to protect her, the staff need to be aware of any unexplained bumps or bruises which might be a sign of further abuse and which they would have to bring to the attention of the officer-in-charge.

Being trustworthy

When someone – a parent or colleague – discloses private information about children and families, obviously you do not gossip about it. This applies equally to what people may raise in the course of meetings and support groups. It takes little imagination to understand how hurtful it would be for your own private business to be discussed by other people. In everyday life some people find it exciting to receive private information and to be able to pass it on and see the effect it has. But people who work with children should think of themselves as professionals, who do not divulge confidential information to third parties. At the same time, it is sometimes professionally necessary to discuss private matters which you have been told about in the course of your work. If you need to do this (we look at the reasons later) you should go to a senior staff member.

- In hospital, a nursery nurse would go to the ward sister.
- Play workers would approach the senior play worker.
- A nursery officer would go to the officer-in-charge.
- An officer-in-charge of a day nursery would go to their manager, as would a senior play worker.

- In school, confide in the headteacher.
- A childminder would go to the social service colleagues with whom they usually liaise.
- Staff in the voluntary sector would go to their line manager.

Passing on information

Talking to senior staff about any information which causes you concern, because of any consequences for a child, is not the same as gossiping. Sometimes it is necessary to pass on confidential information to colleagues for the sake of a child – just as the officer-in-charge in the example given above told staff about the child who had suffered physical abuse. It is something that all staff should be prepared for – a parent will confide in you and you will have to think whether to keep what they say to yourself or to pass it on.

'Need to know'

There are ground rules for deciding when to pass on information about a child, or a family, to other colleagues. Decisions should be made on the basis of whether other staff need to know. Answering the following questions should make it clear whether or not it is necessary to inform colleagues about confidential material:

- Is it necessary to tell colleagues so that they are able to work more effectively with the child or offer a better service to the family?
- Are there dangers for the child or the family if this information is not passed on to other members of staff?

If the answer to either question is 'yes', then the information should be passed on to all those who need it professionally. If you are in a junior position, then you should tell whoever is in charge, who will then decide if it should go any further. If you are given information by a parent that worries or upsets you, it is your duty to discuss it, in confidence, with your boss.

Some day nurseries have a system of 'key workers' by which one person is especially responsible for liaising with one family and is seen as the person who needs to know the relevant information about the family. In other services, all staff who ever work directly with the child concerned are given necessary information. This could include all those who 'cover', that is, act as substitutes, for people who usually work with the child. Decisions about this are made by senior staff.

For example, there is a court order which does not allow Linda's father to have access to her. Linda's mother tells the member of staff in charge of the holiday playscheme that in no circumstances is Linda to be allowed to leave with her father. The senior play worker lets the other two staff know about this, because it is possible that she herself might not be present if the father turned up and the other staff might, unsuspectingly, hand Linda over to him.

Points to discuss or think about

Do you think that it is acceptable for nursery workers to discuss private information about families in any of the following circumstances: in case conferences; at home; over coffee in the staff room; in staff meetings; in discussions during training courses? Can you think of any exceptions to the answers you have given?

Dangers in passing on information

As well as advantages, there are also dangers in passing on information. These include, first and foremost, infringing the privacy of the family concerned: it cannot be stated too strongly or too often that families have a right to privacy and infringing that right should only happen in the real interests of the child.

Second, there is no reason why staff should be burdened with unnecessary details about the families they work with. Some nurseries and family centres only take children whose families are in extremely difficult circumstances – but knowing all the details of the children's backgrounds would be of little help to the nursery workers concerned. Take the example of Cathie, who is on the non-accidental injury register. The local authority social services department expect staff to be alert to any signs of injury. It is, therefore, necessary for the staff to know that Cathie is on the register, so that they do not dismiss any bruising, or other damage, lightly. But there is no need for staff to be told other sensitive material about the family, which could both distress the staff and prejudice their relationship with the family.

So if a mother discloses information about her own unhappy childhood, perhaps in the course of a support group, there is no need for you to pass the information on. It has nothing to do with how you look after her child and no danger will arise because other staff have not been informed. But, once again, if you find that a confidence is upsetting or worrying, you should tell your boss about it. In these circumstances, you should be able to look to whoever is in charge for professional support; this is a way of avoiding undue stress.

Declare you are going to pass information on

If you decide that what you have been told should be made known to others, then you should say so to the person who has confided in you, or who has made disclosures to you or others in a group meeting.

For example, Deidre is a mother of one of the children in your playgroup;

you get on well with her. She tells you that her sister's children, also at the playgroup, are left alone for hours every night while their mother is working at a local pub. She has often heard them crying as she passes the house. She knows that there's a paraffin heater in the bedroom. She has spoken to her sister about it but her sister says that there is nothing she can do – the family needs the money. Deidre says, 'Please don't say anything, I don't want to cause trouble, but I'm worried sick about it.'

This is an awkward position for you, and a situation which could arise for other early years and play workers as well. On the one hand, you believe that there is real danger for the children, on the other you feel loyalty towards Deidre who has confided in you.

In a situation like this, where it seems likely that children are at risk, you have no option but to pass the information on to whoever is your line manager. But you must tell the person who has confided in you that you are going to do so, otherwise they are in a false position. They may believe that you are relating to them in a purely personal way, as a friend, while for you professional responsibilities towards the children have priority. One way forward is to suggest that it would be better for the other person to take the information further themselves. If they are unwilling to do this, you can say that you know it is very difficult for them but that, for the sake of the children, you are going to tell your own line manager about it. If you are working as a childminder, the person to inform would be the social worker who carries out the registration or inspection procedures in your local social services department.

Points to discuss or think about

Read the following, if possible with a partner or in small groups, and decide what you would do. Read over the key points which follow to help you to come to your answer. There may not be one 'right' answer – you may think of different circumstances which would affect what you would do. For example, in the first case, Saleem's mother may have brought him to the nursery that morning.

- Saleem is a three year old at nursery school. One morning, when you are looking at his painting, he says, 'My mum shouted at my dad and she's gone away now.' How do you react? Do you report it to anyone or not? Should you, or a senior worker, 'check out' if what Saleem says is true? What are your reasons for your course of action?
- A mother who has a new baby, brings her older child to the holiday club. She is weeping and says she does not know what to do. She says she is having problems feeding her new baby and that she suffered severe depression after the birth of her first baby. What do you do, if anything, about this information? Why?
- You are an officer-in-charge of a day nursery. Gary's mother tells you that his father has AIDS. To whom – if anyone – do you pass this information? On what grounds do you make this decision?
- You do a home visit to a family where the child, Tom, has just started nursery class. Tom's mother tells you, in confidence, that his father often beats him. What do you say to her and what action, if any, do you take?

CONFIDENTIALITY: KEY POINTS

- Staff who work with children are sometimes given private information about the children and families they work with.
- This information should not be talked about to other parents, nor to anyone who is not professionally concerned with the child or the family.
- Sensitive information should be passed on to other colleagues only if they need to know and in the child's best interests.
- Passing on information infringes the privacy of the people concerned. It can also be a burden for colleagues and one which, in some cases, prejudices staff against a parent.
- If you have any worries about information you have received, pass it on to a senior worker who will then take responsibility for who else, if anyone, should know.
- If you decide that you are going to talk to a senior colleague about a parent's private affairs, you must let the parent know you are going to do this, as part of your professional duty.
- Some employers have their own policy about confidentiality; for example an education authority may have a policy about AIDS or about the non-accidental injury register. A senior colleague can let you know what this is.

14 Interpersonal communication: overview

This chapter takes an overview of interpersonal communication and high-lights some of the main themes and ideas covered in this book.

Effective interpersonal communications are those which best serve the needs of the children. This book has suggested ways in which you can develop inter-personal skills for early years and play work, where all professional skills are, first and foremost, used in the interests of the children. They include practical skills, such as preparing a baby's feed, cleaning a grazed knee or checking the safety of an adventure play structure. Interpersonal skills and your understanding of what happens in interpersonal communication are also for the benefit of the children. This holds for face-to-face communication with the children themselves and for all the interactions with adults, parents and colleagues, which affect the children indirectly. Skills which could affect children indirectly might include, for example, careful listening and re-sponding to a parent's anxieties, or an ability to solve any conflict which might arise with a colleague.

With the children themselves, you can use your skills to:

- *Listen to children.* People are coming to realize that children have a right to be heard. Listening to children shows our respect for them and builds their self-esteem. A willingness to listen to children, and knowing how to do so, is fundamental to effective interpersonal communication with them.
- *Avoid interference.* If you have carried out the observations and exercises described in this book, you will have become aware of everything which interferes with effective communication with children, from using stereo-types to being aware of the part that feelings may play in distorting com-munication.
- *Reflect back.* You have learned that it is often effective to let children know that you have heard what they have said, and understand what they feel, by reflecting back to them. This lets them know that you accept their experience and encourages them to express themselves.
- *Use questions with discrimination and answer children's questions carefully.* Chapter 8 on questions outlined some of the problems that can arise if staff ask children too many questions or have a habit of asking pointless questions. Answering children's questions constructively depends on

being attentive to them and taking what puzzles them seriously.

- *Confront children about unacceptable behaviour, without challenging their self-esteem.* The exercises in Chapters 9 and 11 have provided practice in how to confront the behaviour, rather than the child. Again this is crucial to the child's self-respect.

If you use these skills you will also encourage children to express themselves to the best of their ability and so develop their powers of communication.

Effective communicators can take the other person's point of view. It is an essential interpersonal skill to be able to take the other person's point of view – to listen carefully to what they have to say and to be aware of their non-verbal communications. If you are alert to the many different messages an adult or child is sending, you are in a better position to respond to them. You can, for example, spot that someone is upset – although they do not tell you in so many words – and take this into account in how you respond.

Taking the other person's point of view is necessary in interactions with babies, as well as with adults and older children. From the beginning, babies are individuals with their own experiences and wishes – even if they do not have the ability to put these into words. With babies you need to be sensitive to how they are at any one moment. For example, are they sleepy, fretful, alert or crying? What information do they give about whether they are enjoying a game and are ready for it to be developed further, or want it to stop? Often they take the lead and engage you in play and interaction – but you have to be alert to their signals, to be able to see things from their point of view. If you are, then you know when they are ready for you to take your 'turn' to play, and can time your contribution so that it fits in.

Effective communicators are aware of the part that feelings play in interpersonal communications. Your own and the other person's feelings play a part in all interpersonal communications. If you learn to pay attention to another person's feelings, you can understand their 'messages' more completely. If you become more aware of your own feelings, you are less likely to let them interfere with communication.

Effective communicators respect other people. Respect is shown in many ways, but at its heart is an attitude that the other person has an individual experience of life, that they have their own feelings and ways of understanding and they have the right to be treated equally. This can be shown by trying to understand the other person's point of view and letting them know that you do so, that is, acknowledging their experience, not dismissing or ignoring it. It may be more difficult to do this with some people than with others – it is not possible to like people equally. But, as a professional worker, it is important to take your share of responsibility for making working relationships work. So when there are conflicting interests, you find ways out which meet other people's needs as well as your own; you do not try to control them with blame or judgemental language.

Respect is also shown in how you deal with confidential material. You respect people's right to privacy and only breach confidentiality if a child is in danger – and you tell your informant that you are going to do so.

Similarly, it is a spirit of respect which leads you to avoid stereotyping other people or giving other messages of power and control which keep other people 'in their place' – such a place is always an unequal one. Giving respect to all the people you work with promotes equality for all groups, including those who are oppressed by racism, sexism, disablist practices and other systematic injustice.

In conclusion

Interpersonal communication is going to play an important part in your working life. The skills introduced in *Communicating with Children and Adults* can be developed throughout your career. They are skills which will be of service to parents, to colleagues and, above all, to the many children for whose well-being – physical, social and emotional – you share responsibility.

Useful addresses and further reading

Useful addresses

Afro-Caribbean Education Resource Project (ACER)
Wyvil School, Wyvil Road, London SW8 2TJ
Tel: 0171-627-2662, Fax: 0171-627-0278.

Access to Information on Multi-cultural Education Resources (AIMER)
Bulmershe College of Higher Education, Woodlands Avenue, Earley, Reading RG6 1HY
Tel: 01734-875123 x4871

Centre for Studies on Inclusive Education (CSIE)
1 Redland Close, Elm Lane, Redland, Bristol BS6 6UE
Tel: 0117-923-8450

Children in Scotland (CLANN AN ALBA)
Princes House, 5 Shandwick Place, Edinburgh EH2 4RG

Children's Rights Development Unit
235 Shaftsbury Avenue, London WC2 8EL

Commission for Racial Equality
Elliot House, 10/12 Allington Street, London SW1 5EH
Tel: 0171-828-7022.

Council for Awards in Children's Care and Education
8 Chequer Street, St Albans, Hertfordshire AL1 3XZ

Daycare Trust
4 Wild Court, London WC2B 5AU
Tel: 0171-405-5617

Early Years Trainers Anti-Racist Network (EYTARN)
PO Box 1870, London N12 8JQ
Tel: 0181-446-7056

Equality Learning Centre
356 Holloway Road, London N7 6PA
Tel: 0171-700-8127

Equal Opportunities Commission
Overseas House, Quay Street, Manchester M3 3HN
Tel: 0161-833-9244, Fax: 0161-835-1657

Fair Play For Children
5 Nelson Road, Bognor Regis PO21 2PY

HAPA Adventure Play for Children with Disabilities and Special Needs
Fulham Place, Bishop's Avenue, London SW6 6EA
Tel: 0171-736-4443

Joint National Committee on Training for Playwork
Playbarn, Balaam Street Park, Greengate Street, London E13 0AS

Local Authorities Race Relations Information Exchange
41 Belgrave Square, London SW1 8N2
Tel: 0171-259-5464

MENCAP Early Years Project
123 Golden Lane, London EC1Y 0TJ
Tel: 0171-454-0454

Multi-Cultural Education Resources Centre
66 Cedar Road, Bedford MK42 0JE
Tel: 01234-364475

National Childminding Association
8 Masons Hill, Bromley, Kent BR2 9EY

National Children's Bureau
8 Wakley Street, London EC1V 7QE
Tel: 0171-278-9441

National Early Years Network
77 Holloway Road, London N7 8JZ
Tel: 0171-607-9573

Support and Training Against Racism (STAR)
7 Barton Buildings, Bath, Avon BA1 2JR
Tel: 01225-334415

Voluntary Council for Disabled Children
National Children's Bureau, 8 Wakely Street, London EC1V 7QE
Tel: 0171-843-6000

Working Group Against Racism in Children's Resources
460 Wandsworth Road, London SW8 3LX
Tel: 0171-627-4594

National Centres for Play Work Education contacts

London
Paul Bonel, National Centre for Playwork Education, London
Block D, Barnsbury Park Complex, Offord Road, London N1 1QG

South West
Jacquie Beddows, National Centre for Playwork Education, South West
Cheltenham & Gloucester College of Higher Education, Francis Close Hall,
Swindon Road, Cheltenham GL50 4AZ

North East
Jackie Martin, National Centre for Playwork Education, North East
Kielder House, University of Northumbria, Coach Lane Campus, Benton,
Newcastle upon Tyne NE7 7XA

West Midlands
Jean Elledge, National Centre for Playwork Education, West Midlands
Westhill College, Weoley Park Road, Selly Oak, Birmingham B29 6LL

Other contacts

Playboard Northern Ireland
59–65 York Street, Belfast BT15 1AA

Kids' Club Network
Bellerive House, 3 Muirfield Crescent, London E14 9SZ

National Voluntary Council for Children's Play
National Children's Bureau, 8 Wakley Street, London EC1V 7QE

PLAYLINK
279 Whitechapel Road, London E1 1BY

Play Wales
10–11 Raleigh Walk, Atlantic Wharf, Cardiff CF1 5LN

Pre-school Learning Alliance
61–3 Kings Cross Road, London WC1X 9LL

Scottish Out of School Care Network
55 Renfrew Street, Galsgow G2 3BD

Suggested further reading

Theory
Deaux, K., Dane, F.C., Wrightman, L.S. 1993. *Social Psychology in the 90's,* 6th edition. Brooks/Cole: California (Chapter 5).

Petrie, P. 1994. *Play and Care, Out-of-School.* HMSO.
Richards, M. 1980. *Infancy: World of the Newborn.* Harper and Row: London.
Schaffer, R. 1985. *Mothering.* Fontana: London.
Tizard, B. and Hughes, M. 1984. *Young Children Learning.* Fontana: London.
Wood, D. *et al.,* 1980. *Working with Under Fives.* Grant McIntyre: London.

There are general chapters in other social psychology text books such as Argyle, M. 1981. *Social Skills and Health.* Methuen: London (which apply theory to work situations) or Hargie, O. (ed.) 1986. *A Hand Book of Communication Skills.* Croom Helm: California (especially Chapters 1–10 – an academic approach).

Practice
Nelson-Jones, R. 1993. *Practical Counselling and Helping Skills,* 3rd edition. Cassell: London.

(See also other counselling, helping, and human relationship skills titles by this author.)

Equality
Brown, B. 1990. *All Our Children: A Guide for Those Who Care.* BBC Publications: London.
Checklist for Accessible Play. HAPA: London
Kapasi, H. 1992. *Asian Children Play.* PLAY-TRAIN: Birmingham.
Lane, J. 1995. *From Cradle to School.* Commission for Racial Equality: London.

Index

messages *cont.*
  indirect 14, 74–5, 76
  receiving 10, 12, 25
  sending 6, 25, 72
movements and gestures 15, 17

'need to know' 117–18
non-verbal communication 2, 6–15, 37,
    41, 50, 88, 96
  body language 12–15
  distance 15
  facial expression 10–12, 88
  frown 11, 41, 50
  gaze 10, 19, 33
  movements and gestures 15, 17, 88
  orientation 14–15
  smiling 10, 19, 41
  touch 2, 12–13, 16
  vocalization 8–9, 42, 88
    non-verbal sounds 9, 42
    pitch 9, 42
    stress 9

observations 2–4
orientation of body 14–15

partings 52–3
Petrie, P. 70
Pinney, R. 45
preverbal communication 2, 17–24
problem solving 101, *see also* win/win

questions 2, 4, 39, 44, 62–71, 99, 121
  asking children 2, 22, 67
  children's 2, 29–30, 68
  closed 62–3, 67, 112
  for clarification 63, 64, 66
  helpful 64–5
  open 62, 63, 112, 113
  responsibilities arising from asking 66
  sensitive 49, 66
  too many 36, 65

questions *cont.*
  to show interest 35, 63–4
racism 2, 80–3, 93, 99
reflecting back 43, 44, 45–6, 51, 53, 54, 60,
    64, 65, 67, 82, 88, 121
respect 122–3
rituals, in nursery 21
Rubin, J. Z *et al.* 79

sad events 55
Schaffer, R. 47
Seavey, C. *et al.* 79
self-esteem 26, 72, 73
setting boundaries
  adults 100
  children 99–100
sensitive questions 49, 66
sexism 2, 76, 77, 93
sharing experience 59
smiling 6, 19, 41, 50
social control 2, 78–84
special needs, *see* disability
'special times' 45–6
speech, clear 33–4
'state' of baby 22
stereotypes 75–7

telephone, communicating by 42
Tizard, B. 67
touch 6, 12–13, 16
  unwanted touch 13–14
trust 116–17
turn-taking 22, 60

United Nations Convention on the
    Rights of the Child 26
vocalization 8–9, 42, 88

win/win 87, 91, 101
Wood, D. 67

'you' language 98